Baggage Claim

Counsel That Helps Others
to Recover Themselves

I owe a great debt of gratitude to my editorial advisor, Mr. Matthew Sheehy, who has labored countless hours to make my thoughts and my heart clear to my readers. Matthew Sheehy was born in New York City. He graduated from the SUNY College of Environmental Science and Forestry at Syracuse University in 1997 with a B.S. in chemistry. He then attended Duke University in Durham, North Carolina, with the intention of earning a Ph.D. in chemistry. Upon being called to the ministry under the preaching of Dr. Rick Finley at Fellowship Baptist Church, he left Duke University with an M.S. degree and moved to Northwest Indiana. He began attending the First Baptist Church of Hammond, Indiana, and Hyles-Anderson College in 2000. Matthew graduated from Hyles-Anderson in 2003 with a master's degree in pastoral theology. For the past five years, he has served as a Bible teacher and as the academic advisor at Hammond Baptist High School. Matthew married his wife, Amy, on July 24, 1999. They now reside in Crown Point, Indiana.

BAGGAGE CLAIM

A Manual on Counseling That Helps Others
to Recover Themselves

DR. JACK SCHAAP

COPYRIGHT © 2009
Hyles Publications

1st Printing – March 2009

ISBN: 0-9800594-8-8

All Scripture quotations are from the King James Bible.

CREDITS
Project Manager: Dr. Bob Marshall
Assistant: Rochelle Chalifoux
Transcription: Cyndilu Marshall
Page Design and Layout: Linda Stubblefield
Proofreading: Debbie Borsh, Kelly Cervantes,
Rena Fish

To order additional books by Dr. Jack Schaap,
please contact:
HYLES PUBLICATIONS
523 Sibley Street
Hammond, Indiana 46320
www.hylespublications.com
e-mail: info@hylespublications.com

Dedication

Affectionally dedicated to the teachers of the Adult Sunday School classes at First Baptist Church, who have joined me as spiritual coaches to help those in trouble to recover themselves and to restore them to a life of victory and spiritual success.

About the Author

Dr. Jack Schaap is the senior pastor of First Baptist Church of Hammond, Indiana, recognized as one of the largest congregations in America. He has a B.S., an M.Ed., and a D.D. from Hyles-Anderson College in Crown Point, Indiana.

Dr. Schaap counsels approximately 100 church members weekly; he superintends more than 3,000 Christian young people in five separate church-operated, private Christian schools, including one in China. Dr. Schaap is the chancellor of Hyles-Anderson College, a private Bible college which First Baptist Church operates for the purpose of training preachers, missionaries, and Christian educators. For more than 20 years, he preached 35 yearly meetings to tens of thousands of teenagers. First Baptist Church has the largest children's and teens' ministries in America. Dr. Schaap is the author of 17 books and several pamphlets.

Dr. Schaap has been married to his wife Cindy since 1979, and they have two adult children who serve in the ministries of First Baptist Church.

Endorsements

As a young preacher I was taught that a sermon is a greasy wrench that you use to fix something. For the past 30 years I have been adding other "tools" to my ministry "toolbox." As my ministry has grown, and as the lives of people have become more complex, I have found an ever-increasing need for me to become better equipped to help them.

Dr. Schaap's book on counseling has not only helped me to be a more effective counselor, it has challenged me to share this ministry "tool" with other leaders in my church. As others learn to wield this tool effectively, my influence will be broadened, my load will be lightened, and I will be able to help more and more people whose broken lives need to be "fixed."

> – Pastor Rick Finley
> Fellowship Baptist Church
> Durham, North Carolina

In this wonderful book on Biblical counseling, Dr. Jack Schaap has provided a Bible-based, extremely practical and richly insightful work on the responsibilities and duties of every

Christian counselor. He has given such valuable truths that irrespective of whether someone has counseled for many years, or is just embarking on the ministry of counseling and mentoring, there will be a great benefit in studying this book.

Reading this book has helped me bring new insight to the ministry of counseling that I am personally engaged in every day. Read this book, carefully incorporate its great truths, and be prepared for God to have your counseling begin to make a dramatic impact on the lives of those whom you desire to help.

I highly recommend this book to everyone who desires to truly help others in their Christian walk. I consider this book a must-read for anyone who desires to have God make his counseling useful and effective for the cause of Christ!

– Attorney David Gibbs, Jr., Founder
Christian Law Association

In this book Brother Schaap works his way through the minefield of pastoral counseling. He warns of the dangers that face those who take on the responsibility of counseling God's people. He also charts a course that, if followed, will repair the damaged lives of those seeking counsel. Solid Biblical counsel is here for both the aspiring counselor and the experienced one. I thoroughly enjoyed reading this great contribution to counseling among our independent, fundamental Baptist brethren.

– Dr. Les Hobbins, Pastor Emeritus
Lewis Avenue Baptist Church
Temperance, Michigan

I have completed reading the transcript of Dr. Schaap's book on counseling. What a help! I heartily recommend this book to leaders everywhere who want their influence to count for Christ. In my 32 years of pastoring, I have counseled thousands. How I wish this resource had been available from my start! We will likely be incorporating this book into our college for preacher boys especially as they prepare for the ministry as pastors and missionaries.

My heartfelt thanks goes to Dr. Schaap for helping all of us in the field have the best tools possible as we work to build for Christ.

– Dr. John R. Morgan
International Baptist Church
Brooklyn, New York

It is easy for me, as well as a great joy for me, to recommend Dr. Jack Schaap's book on counseling. Many of the things that the Lord has given me over the years are embodied in these pages. I praise the Lord for giving Dr. Schaap the ability to write in such a practical way the helps that so many need to know in order to help others. The challenge in this book to get wisdom from the Lord is so needed today.

I have seen thousands of signs, "Pray for power," but never have I seen "Give me the wisdom to use the power." By reading this book you will understand the wise man does not believe himself to be wise, but knows how and where to obtain wisdom. I encourage you to purchase this book as a powerful guide to bring you and those you help to the counseling of the blessed old Book of Books.

– Evangelist Tom Williams, President
Tom Williams Worldwide Ministries

Contents

CHAPTER ONE

The Biblical Purpose for Counseling

Growing churches eventually reach a saturation point that bottlenecks growth. The excitement of fulfilling the Great Commission is contagious in a growing church. Momentum is gained through the zeal of the church members. However, the results of enthusiasm and growth often become the church's own worst enemy. A growing church must develop a plan to meet every person's spiritual needs. Churches which do not implement a plan eventually reach a plateau, stagnate through frustration, and decline in attendance.

A bottleneck is a backup on a highway caused by a reduction in the number of lanes. As three lanes of highway become one, drivers move into the only open lane. A bottleneck can cause a backup that is several miles long and impede the progress of all of the cars on the highway. A bottleneck is analogous to the halted growth in a stagnant church.

Proverbs 1:5

"A wise man will hear, and will increase learning; and a man of understanding shall attain unto wise counsels."

Proverbs 15:22,

"Without counsel purposes are disappointed: but in the multitude of counsellers they are established."

Proverbs 1:5, *"A wise man will hear, and will increase learning; and a man of understanding shall attain unto wise counsels."* Proverbs 15:22, *"Without counsel purposes are disappointed: but in the multitude of counsellers they are established."*

Church members must be trained to accommodate the growth in numbers of people so that every problem does not have to go through the pastor. Both Proverbs 1:5 and 15:22 teach that there should be a number of counselors in a man's life. Thus, the pastor cannot be the only man who is available to give people Biblical wisdom. Everyone has only 24 hours in a day, so a pastor is limited in the number of problems he can help. There is a limit on how many people a pastor can shepherd, and every man has a different number. If a pastor has a limit of 100 people, he might quickly build a church of 100. The observer will then notice that the church will stagnate. For every person that joins, someone else leaves because he is not finding the necessary help.

Numbers 11 describes how God told Moses to gather 70 elders of Israel unto whom Moses' spirit would be imparted. Moses' spirit was placed on them to help bear the burden of the people. When God took the spirit of Moses and gave it to the 70 elders at the tabernacle, they began to prophesy. Two of the seventy were not at the tabernacle for the event but remained in the camp. The spirit of Moses was still given to them, and they also started prophesying. One particular young man heard these two men prophesying and worried that they had the audacity to emulate what Moses did. The young man ran to tell his leader. When Joshua heard the report, he said to Moses, *"...My lord Moses, forbid them."* (Numbers 11:28)

In the following verse Moses wisely replied, *"...Enviest thou for my sake? would God that all the LORD's people were prophets, and that the LORD would put his spirit upon them!"* Moses understood that he could not do all of the work; these 70 men would assist him in caring for the burdens of the people.

Bible-believing churches need to disavow the common idea of a clergy-laity structure. The pastor does not have unique access to God. He does not perform a religious show for a cathedral of spectators. The pastor should possess the spirit of God and desire that men in his church receive the same spirit. Churches should not be filled with spectators, but with spiritual leaders who are properly trained and empowered to assist in pastoral care.

The wise pastor will set up a Biblically based system of training his men to train other men. A pastor can identify a spiritual man in his church and mentor him on handling certain problems. He can teach spiritual men how to match scriptural answers with complex problems. The spiritual man might be able to handle mentoring and caring for ten people. This may not seem like much, but the pastor has now increased the potential of his church to 110 people. If the pastor could train

5 men in his church to mentor 10 people, his church's potential has grown to 150 members.

If everyone in a church has to see the pastor when a problem arises, then the church can only grow to the potential of the pastor. As a church grows, the pastor needs to devote more of his time to Bible study and prayer. The time available to counsel diminishes, yet the need to counsel grows. Churches need men who will accept the challenge of growing the church through aiding the pastor. Churches need men who will accept the challenge of mentoring, whether or not they receive a paycheck.

Jesus said in Luke 14:13, 14, *"But when thou makest a feast, call the poor, the maimed, the lame, the blind:* [14]*And thou shalt be blessed; for they cannot recompense thee: for thou shalt be recompensed at the resurrection of the just."* As a church follows the Biblical model to reach the poor, they will need to offer help in marriages, finances, child rearing, addictions, and dealing with emotional baggage. The pastor cannot possibly handle all of these problems. Churches are spiritual hospitals, and one doctor can't handle all of the patients because they will have diminished care, diminished follow-up, or will die before they can be examined.

The pastor of a church with sustained growth will train people to assist him. Churches need to develop a strong mentoring program. Counseling is essentially mentoring; a counselor adopts a person and invests his life in him.

Mentors are needed in a church because many hearers of the Word are unable to assimilate the truths. Many people sleep or daydream through preaching. Some people serve God in a ministry such as a children's church service or in the nursery and, as a result, do not hear the preaching. Every problem is solvable through the Word of God, but some people will not grasp the concept until a concerned mentor individually shows them how to apply Biblical principles to solve the problem.

A Christian who tries to avoid the world is like a man trying to run between raindrops without getting wet. Living in this world afflicts people's spirits. Christians carry the wounds from relationships, defilement, unclean minds, anger, bitterness, strife, contention, pride, and lust.

Marriage is the one relationship in life where these wounds become weapons. A man and a woman enter marriage with the utmost ideals and expectations; they are expecting a utopia of heavenly bliss. But those emotional scars brew, then percolate into festering wounds, and eventually spew hot, blistering, scalding words and actions.

Nothing in our culture is as destructive as an unbiblical family structure, which includes divorced homes, single-parent homes, cohabitation of unmarried couples, and same-sex relationships. The National Marriage Project describes itself as a "nonpartisan, nonsectarian and interdisciplinary initiative located at Rutgers, the State University of New Jersey...to provide research and analysis on the state of marriage in America and to educate the public on the social, economic and cultural conditions affecting marital success and well-being."[1] In their "The State of our Unions 2007" report, the introduction states the following:

Long-term trends point to the gradual weakening of marriage as the primary social institution of family life. More Americans today are living together, marrying at older ages or not at all, and rearing children in cohabiting or solo parent households. The weakening of marriage is attributed to a broad cultural shift away from religion and social traditionalism and toward faith in personal independence and tolerance for diverse lifestyles—otherwise known as 'secular individualism.' This cultural shift is a central feature of modern societies and therefore unlikely to be reversed...it will probably require a cultural awakening, perhaps prompted by rational self-interest, to avoid such an outcome. We will have to adopt the view that personal happiness depends on high-trust and lasting relationships and that such relationships require constraints on short-term adult interests in order to foster long-term commitments to children, and thus to the future.[2]

The "cultural awakening" that is needed will not successfully be prompted by "rational self-interest"; it will be prompted by a spiritual awakening founded on Scripture. Challenge yourself to be a counselor and mentor. *Counselor* is a Biblical word; *mentor* is a modern word. These words have similar meanings and will be used interchangeably throughout the book. This manual is devoted to teaching spiritual people how to mentor and counsel people to stop the bleeding, suture the wound, and manage the scars. A church must develop a program to make as many people as possible capable of helping the church members build Biblically stable homes.

Counselors must study and become comfortable and competent with the Scriptures so they can help other people solve their own basic problems. Few things will keep a man on his toes and stir him to spiritual action more than having to teach the Bible to others. A counselor will learn much about the Christian life if he is helping other people with their problems.

People need to connect with the Word of God and avail themselves of the mind of Christ so they can deliver themselves from their own problems and then be used to mentor other people.

[1]"State of Our Unions 2007: The Future of Marriage in America," The National Marriage Project.

[2]*Ibid.*

CHAPTER TWO

Why People Need a Counselor

Pe018e who seek counsel usually do not have a good idea of their true problem, so a counselor needs to help them see the conflict. The person seeking counsel will often insist that he knows why the problem exists, but his reason is usually not Biblical; thus, he doesn't know the true problem. People seeking counsel expect results, so counselors diagnose the symptoms and offer solutions.

Cynical responses are common to a counselor's advice because many people seeking counsel believe they have the problem figured out before they meet with the counselor. (Many people see a counselor to appease a spouse or family member instead of to seek a solution.) The cynicism is a result of their resistance to the Biblical model for counseling. People who need counsel rarely think that the problem lies within themselves; instead, they generally point their finger of blame at another. People need a counselor to teach them how to change themselves when they want to blame outside sources.

Timothy was mentored by the Apostle Paul. The two men preached the Gospel, built churches, and wrote epistles. When they were not together, it was because Paul entrusted Timothy to oversee a ministry while he continued elsewhere. The Bible contains two letters that Paul wrote to Timothy that have been labeled "pastoral epistles" because within them Paul gives advice to his protégé on how to be a man of God and Biblically serve people.

Three verses containing advice that is pertinent to mentoring and counseling are found in II Timothy 2:24-26, which says, *"And the servant of the Lord must not strive; but be gentle unto all men, apt to teach, patient, 25In meekness instructing those that oppose themselves; if God peradventure will give them repentance to the acknowledging of the truth; 26And that they may recover themselves out of the snare of the devil, who are taken captive by him at his will."* From this passage comes a four-fold plan for counseling:

The Purpose:	The person seeking counsel must recover himself from the snare of the Devil.
The Plan:	The counselor must know what to teach and instruct that a man may recover himself.
The Problem:	The person seeking counsel must realize that his ultimate problem is himself.
The Procedure:	The person seeking counsel must acknowledge the truth and implement the plan.

The Purpose ——

The goal of counseling is to help the one seeking counsel to recover himself. A good counselor ultimately eliminates his own job because he teaches the person how to handle a problem by himself. A counselor should not make any person asking for counsel dependent upon him. A counselor teaches a man to make his own decisions. The counselor leads a man to believe in his heart that God is his necessity.

Parenting is a classic example of teaching a person to recover himself. As parents rear a boy, they ultimately want him to be mature enough to leave home and support a wife. They guide their son to an independent adulthood. Strife arises in the home when a child is not being trained to be an independent adult. Ultimately, the counselor leads the one he is counseling to be independent of others, but dependent on God.

The Plan ——

II Timothy 2:24 says a counselor (*"the servant of the Lord"*) teaches and instructs. Timothy was instructed to commit to faithful men the truths that Paul taught him. *"And the things that thou hast heard of me among many witnesses, the same commit thou to faithful men, who shall be able to teach others also."* (II Timothy 2:2) The things which Timothy heard were many of the New Testament words that were penned by Paul. Today men should still be teaching the words of the Bible to other men. The person seeking counsel needs a proven Scriptural plan to recover himself.

Proverbs 1:5 says, *"A wise man will hear, and will increase learning; and a man of understanding shall attain unto wise counsels."* The Hebrew word for *counsel* (*tachbulah*) in this verse describes how the sailors on a shipping vessel manage the ropes in order to manipulate the masts and steer the ship. Massive sailboats contain dozens of ropes that alter the position of the sails. A good sailor notes the wind's direction and adjusts the sails with the ropes so that the vessel can stay on course. Counselors must discern from which direction pressure is being applied and have a plan to direct the person seeking counsel to the proper destination.

A counselor must have a plan. Proverbs 1:25 says, *"But ye have set at nought all my counsel, and would none of my reproof."* The Hebrew word for *counsel* (`*etsah*) in this verse refers to a plan. Ironically, this verse was written from Solomon to his son, Rehoboam, who ultimately rejected the wise plan of older men, chose the foolish plan of younger men, and divided the kingdom. Counseling is not merely listening—although that comforts people—and throwing out some ideas. A counselor guides people to and through a plan. A counselor pulls the ropes in a person's life to steer him toward a goal.

Each time the book of Proverbs refers to a *counselor,* the word has been translated from the Hebrew word *ya`ats* which means "to advise or resolve." Counseling puts courage into people. A counselor resolves a problem by breaking the plan down into manageable steps. The overall plan might be overwhelming to some people, but they can be encouraged when the counselor explains the smaller steps that will accomplish the plan.

The counselor's opinion does not constitute a plan.

People who call themselves counselors but have no plan to follow make two common mistakes:

- They give their opinion.
- They display a sympathetic ear.

Counseling does not occur when a counselor offers his personal opinion. God has prescribed plans in the Bible for marriage, child rearing, finances, overcoming addictions and sins, and building relationships. A counselor needs to know these plans and lead the one seeking counsel to the correct plan. A counselor points to the Bible and tells people where God wants to steer the ship.

Offering a sympathetic ear does not constitute a plan. Caring deeply does not qualify a person to be a good counselor, although empathy is a quality worth possessing. Counselors may weep and get teary-eyed, but sympathy and empathy are temporary balms; they are not the tools to self-recovery. Sympathy and empathy are the ties to dependency. Comfort and counsel can be confused by well-intentioned people, but the true counselor lays out a plan for someone to follow.

Counselors make a mistake when they give their own plan and play God. The plan should come from God, but counselors do not play God. No counselor can tell the person who is seeking his counsel what is God's unknown will. The Bible is filled with the known will of God, but it does not tell anyone the exact person to marry, what career he should seek, or where he should live. The Bible gives direction on how to make these choices, but nowhere does it say, "Bill Smith is to study medicine, marry Jane Jones, and live in Gulfport,

Mississippi." Strife happens because a counselor who wants to play God in the life of the person seeking his counsel feels rejected if his plan is not followed. The wise counselor says, "I can only tell you the Bible plan, and then you can take up the matter with God. Here are some options for implementing that truth. Whether or not you do is up to you." If a counselor has this attitude, he will never strive with another.

People seeking counsel need a counselor to help them choose a plan. The Biblical plan that the counselor presents contains which truths to apply, how to apply them, and where to apply them. Counselors must avoid being deep, instead laying the building blocks of Biblical principles. Just as a construction worker chooses a hammer when a nail needs to be driven, the counselor must know how to discern which Biblical truths and plans should be applied to the life of the person seeking his counsel. He must then teach the individual how to apply Biblical principles to other areas of his life. Many people have the ability to do exactly what they are told; they can take advice for a specific situation and solve the problem. However, they do not know how to apply the same principles to a slightly different situation. A good counselor teaches the plans to apply, how to apply them, and how to discern or understand modified situations where they can be applied.

The Problem ——

The counselor is teaching and training a person to self-realize that he opposes himself, and this struggle is the core problem of all counseling. When people are at war, they will point fingers at others, but they must ultimately realize that they are opposing themselves and not other people. The Bible says in Ephesians 6:12, *"For we wrestle not against flesh and blood..."*; thus, the ultimate war is never with another person; the problem is between a person and the power of darkness. When a counselor leads the person seeking counsel to perform his own responsibilities, the other problems tend to fall in line.

The Procedure ——

Counselors help people acknowledge the truth, and this is the hardest part of counseling. Most people are quicker to admit they are wrong than to acknowledge the truth. An individual will often admit that he is wrong just to get the counselor off his back. A person can admit he is a sinner, but he is not saved until he acknowledges the truth of the Gospel. A person does not begin to recover until he can honestly say in his heart, "I have wrong thinking, and I need to change the way I think about this." The person seeking counsel needs to look at the plan presented by the counselor and agree that it is the Bible truth.

One struggle in counseling is getting people to see the truth. If the person does not see that the counselor's plan is filled with wisdom, then the counselor is wasting his time. The one seeking counsel needs enough sense to listen to the counselor.

The plan cannot be forced upon the one needing counsel. A counselor does not argue as he teaches and trains because the servant of the Lord does not strive. If a counselor understands the concept of a person's recovering himself, he finds striving unnecessary because he cannot recover anyone else. The counselor does not order, "You do what I tell you to do!" Instead, he presents the plan and then patiently and meekly instructs and encourages the one who has come to him for counsel to follow through. Soul winning is a great example of this concept because the soul winner presents the Gospel, gives an opportunity to receive the truth, and allows the sinner to make a personal decision with God.

The counselor patiently watches the person's progress with the plan because a counselor is called to be patient, gentle, and meek if the one seeking his counsel is to recover himself. A counselor puts up with the problems and interruptions that sidetrack the plan. No person should be a counselor if he cannot cope with having a bomb dropped on him and his plan. Counselors must have their shock absorbers installed at all times.

If people are to acknowledge the truth, they sometimes have to be confronted with the truth. Ephesians 4:14, 15 says, *"That we henceforth be no more children, tossed to and fro, and carried about with every wind of doctrine, by the sleight of men, and cunning craftiness, whereby they lie in wait to deceive; 15But speaking the truth in love, may grow up into him in all things, which is the head, even Christ."* Those who seek counsel might be children who are "tossed to and fro." Paul instructed the Ephesians to speak the truth in love to these people that they might grow up as Christians. The truth hurts and can sometimes be confrontational. A counselor will need to be confrontational at times, but he does not strive. Confrontation does not have to involve a fight; it involves an obvious presentation of the truth.

Looking someone in the eye and saying, "According to the Bible, you are wrong," can be difficult, but people need to hear that from their counselor. It is even harder to say, "You are wrong," in love and have the person who has come to you for counsel believe that you still love him.

The outline for counseling described in this chapter is very broad; it merely provides the basics of counseling according to one Bible passage. For each person seeking counsel, you will have to diagnose the symptoms and offer a plan unique to his life. That is no easy feat unless you have wisdom as discussed in the next chapter.

CHAPTER THREE

The Wisdom of a Counselor

Possessing the wisdom of God is essential for a counselor to properly diagnose symptoms and offer solutions for a unique conflict. College degrees and IQ neither qualify nor disqualify a person from being a counselor. Knowledge is important, but knowledge is useless unless the counselor knows how to use it. Wisdom engenders success to its users regardless of height, weight, gender, race, intelligence, or strength.

Simply stated, wisdom is applied knowledge. Wisdom involves discerning and judging that which is the most just, proper, and useful in a situation. A wise person can make unique applications of his knowledge to unique situations.

God is the only source of all true wisdom. Proverbs 2:6 says, *"For the LORD giveth wisdom: out of his mouth cometh knowledge and understanding."* The quest is to obtain wisdom from God; the quandary is how to procure it from Him.

The prophet Daniel received wisdom from God as he stated in Daniel 2:23. *"I thank thee, and praise thee, O thou God of my fathers, who hast given me wisdom and might, and hast made known unto me now what we desired of thee: for thou hast now made known unto us the king's matter."* Daniel was faced with execution because none of the Babylonian magicians, astrologers, or sorcerers could tell King Nebuchadnezzar the details of his forgotten dream. Like many dreams that seem so real, the king's dream vanished when he awoke. The dream startled him, so he called his counselors and asked them to interpret the dream. When the counselors asked Nebuchadnezzar for the details of the dream, the king replied that he did not remember them. Still, he demanded that the counselors tell him the dream's contents and meaning. They replied that no king ever demanded such an impossible task. The king then said that if they truly were wise men, then they should be able to know the details of his dream. Since they admitted that they could not tell Nebuchadnezzar what he dreamed, the king reasoned that they must not be as wise as they proclaimed. His conclusion was to rid the kingdom of these fraudulent wise men.

Unfortunately for Daniel, he was considered one of the wise men, although he had not stood before the king on that day. When Daniel saw the order being hastily carried out, he asked why it was so. He was informed of the situation by the king's captain. Daniel successfully petitioned the king for a temporary reprieve and an opportunity to discover the dream and its interpretation.

Daniel asked his three companions, Hananiah, Mishael, and Azariah, to pray that God would reveal the dream. In a night-time vision, Daniel understood the dream and interpretation. They had asked God for the counsel that was needed to appease King Nebuchadnezzar, and they received it. Upon receiving the answered prayer, Daniel praised God for the wisdom received as stated in Daniel 2:20-23, *"Daniel answered and said, Blessed be the name of God for ever and ever: for wisdom and might are his: 21And he changeth the times and the seasons: he removeth kings, and setteth up kings: he giveth wisdom unto the wise, and knowledge to them that know understanding: 22He revealeth the deep and secret things: he knoweth what is in the darkness, and the light dwelleth with him. 23I thank thee, and praise thee, O thou God of my fathers, who hast given me wisdom and might, and hast made known unto me now what we desired of thee: for thou hast now made known unto us the king's matter."*

Proverbs 2:6 and Daniel's song agree: wisdom is God's, and He grants it to whomever He chooses. A counselor needs to be the person to whom God grants wisdom. The text from Daniel gives a clue on how to be the recipient of wisdom. Daniel said, *"...he giveth wisdom unto the wise...."* If a counselor is to receive wisdom, he must first be wise.

The conditions sound impossible! If an individual wants to obtain wisdom, he must already be wise. Why would someone need to obtain wisdom if he is already wise? If a man were unwise, how would he then obtain wisdom? On the surface, it appears to be a vicious cycle. The situation is similar to borrowing money from a bank. If a shabby-looking man has no assets and is broke, the bank won't give him a loan even though he needs money. However, if a sharply dressed man with many assets and great credit walks into the bank, he will be given a loan. He has money and knows how to use it; thus, the bank trusts him with their money.

The answer to the wisdom quandary is as simple as understanding the bank analogy. God reveals new wisdom to the counselor when the counselor already does what he knows is wise. God explained wisdom throughout the Bible, and He concentrated its teaching in the book of Proverbs. If the counselor wants to be wise, he should study and copy the actions of wise people because God will then treat him as a wise man. The man who wants to be wise will study the book of Proverbs (and other passages on wisdom) to see what wise men do. The remainder of this chapter is devoted to studying what wise men do according to the Bible. The list is not complete, so the man that truly wants to be a wise counselor will take the initiative to further study wisdom.

1. A wise man asks for wisdom. James 1:5 says, *"If any of you lack wisdom, let him ask of God, that giveth to all men liberally, and upbraideth not; and it shall be given him."* God liberally gives wisdom to those who ask. God doesn't scold anyone who asks for wisdom; He just gives it to the person asking.

King Solomon is an excellent Biblical example of a man's success in asking for wisdom. Solomon knew that he needed wisdom beyond his current capacity when he followed the reign of his father, David, the greatest king in the history of Israel. The Bible says that the people *"...saw that the wisdom of God was* in him..." (I Kings 3:28) and that "...God gave Solomon wisdom...." (I Kings 4:29) Solomon received this wisdom by asking for it as recorded in II Chronicles 1:7-12. God offered Solomon whatever his heart desired. Solomon asked for wisdom and knowledge so that he could judge the people. God granted the request and added unparalleled riches, wealth, and honor.

Solomon's wisdom was exhibited when he had to judge between two women who disputed over the custody of a baby. The story is a great example of counseling in the Bible. Solomon had to settle a dispute, though he had not previously faced this situation. He applied his knowledge of a mother's love for her child and used that to discern the answer.

Requesting wisdom results in receiving wisdom. Daniel and Solomon are two examples of God's fulfilling His promise in James 1 to give wisdom to those who ask. The third example will be the wise counselor who asks God for the wisdom that he needs to show off God—as Daniel did—or to judge between people—as Solomon exemplified. God will liberally give wisdom once a person is qualified, but He circumspectly decides to whom it is granted.

2. A wise man listens. Proverbs 1:5 says, *"A wise man will hear, and will increase learning; and a man of understanding shall attain unto wise counsels."* If a person wants wisdom, then he must be a good listener. Listening increases learning, and what is learned might be rightly applied to help someone. The listening by a wise man might also apply to listening to the one seeking counsel so that the counselor can understand the entire truth as he judges a situation. If the counselor expects people to listen to him, then God expects the counselor to be a listener.

3. A wise man walks uprightly. Proverbs 2:7 says, *"He layeth up sound wisdom for the righteous: he is a buckler to them that walk uprightly."* A person who walks uprightly is someone who walks innocently or walks with honesty. The man who will receive wisdom has integrity.

Wisdom is the character of completeness. When it is said of a man, "There is just something missing about that person; he doesn't get it," the speaker means that the man lacks wisdom because a wise man is a complete man. *Integrity* comes from the word *integer* which refers to a whole number in mathematics. An integer is a complete number. The man who walks uprightly has integrity and is complete.

A wise man sees the complete picture. He is not one-dimensional; rather, he is a fully dimensioned person. Counseling requires that the counselor see the whole picture. A person is a poor counselor when he willfully or ignorantly sees only one side of the argument. When a man sees all sides of an issue, he can then use his wisdom to make a complete assessment.

When God decides on whom He will bestow wisdom, He is looking for an honest man because that man won't waste God's wisdom. That man won't spend God's wisdom on something foolish. God believes that man will use his wisdom to help someone else. God doesn't want to give His wisdom to a man who will not be walking uprightly within a few years. The man who has integrity has no limit to wisdom as long as he is wise enough to keep requesting wisdom as mentioned in James 1.

4. A wise man controls his tongue. Wisdom is the character of control. Proverbs 15:2 says, *"The tongue of the wise useth knowledge aright: but the mouth of fools poureth out foolishness."* The wise man does not have words pouring out of his mouth. He does not say whatever comes to the cusp of his lips. Proverbs 10:8 says, *"The wise in heart will receive commandments: but a prating fool shall fall."* A prating fool is someone who talks too much. The man who does too much talking is not a man displaying wisdom. Proverbs 10:19 says, *"In the multitude of words there wanteth not sin: but he that refraineth his lips is wise."* The wise man refrains his lips; *refrain* is a word of control.

Proverbs does not warn a man about what he looks at with his eyes, listens to with his ears, or touches with his hands as much as it mentions what he says with his tongue. What a man does with his eyes, ears, and hands can disqualify him from receiving wisdom, but the tongue is the most important body part to control if he wants to obtain wisdom. James 1 says that if any man can control the tongue, he can control the entire body. Thus, if he controls the timing, content, and tenor of his words, he can control the lusts of his eyes, ears, and hands.

Proverbs contains many warnings about critics and scorners. What a man says about others limits his potential to receive wisdom. Proverbs 14:6 says, *"A scorner seeketh wisdom, and findeth it not: but knowledge is easy unto him that understandeth."* A scorner is a person who despises with his words; he scoffs at religion and authority. This verse proves that God does not give wisdom to the scoffer, a man who cannot control his tongue.

5. A wise man chooses good companions. Proverbs 13:20 says, *"He that walketh with wise men shall be wise: but a companion of fools shall be destroyed."* God judges a person's wisdom by the crowd with which he is associated. Proverbs 7:4, 5 says, *"Say unto wisdom, Thou art my sister; and call understanding thy kinswoman:* 5*That they may keep thee from the strange woman, from the stranger which flattereth with her words."* God teaches that a man should be around the family (sister, kinswoman) of wise people. The crowd with whom a man makes friends is an indicator of his heart and his future. If a person chooses unwise companions, God sees that man's future without much wisdom. Thus, God will not bestow His wisdom on the man with a foolish future.

6. A wise man is obedient to his father. God observes how a man reacts to his father. Proverbs 23:19 says, *"Hear thou, my son, and be wise, and guide thine heart in the way."* God says that a man displays wisdom when he hears what his father says. The phrase *"my son"* appears 23 times in the book of Proverbs. Each instance is a chance for the son to display wisdom when he hears and increases learning. Each instance is an opportunity for the son to prove to God that he will copy the acts of wise men so that he may receive even more wisdom. A father sires his child, feeds his child, protects his child, and provides for his child. If the child is not smart enough to accept the wisdom of that man, then God sees that the child is void of wisdom and will not give him more wisdom.

7. A wise man acquires advice from good sources. The 23 occurrences of *"my son"* in Proverbs are all evidences of taking advice. A father is usually a good source of wisdom. Proverbs is filled with opportunities for a young man to receive advice from a wise father. Proverbs 12:15 says, *"The way of a fool is right in his own eyes: but he that hearkeneth unto counsel is wise."* The wise man is aware that he is not omniscient. The wise man knows that his ways are not the best ways. The wise man looks to others who might have wisdom in an area where he is lacking.

Another Biblical example of seeking good advice is found in Proverbs 19:20 which says, *"Hear counsel, and receive instruction, that thou mayest be wise in thy latter end."* Proverbs 20:18 says, *"Every purpose is established by counsel: and with good advice make war."* When a wise man has tough decisions to make, he will run his ideas by other wise men. God wants to see if a man has enough humility to have others veto his ideas. A man can get an idea in his head and not consider many of its pitfalls because he is bedazzled by the possibilities for success. God wants to see if a man is wise enough to avoid potential pitfalls by seeking the advice of other wise men. When God sees a man seek this advice, He is ready to give greater wisdom to that man.

8. The wise man avoids immorality. Proverbs 5:1-4 says, *"My son, attend unto my wisdom, and bow thine ear to my understanding: ²That thou mayest regard discretion, and that thy lips may keep knowledge. ³For the lips of a strange woman drop as an honeycomb, and her mouth is smoother than oil: ⁴But her end is bitter as wormwood, sharp as a twoedged sword."* Solomon explicitly instructed his son to avoid the immoral woman; he instructed his son that there was wisdom in avoiding such a woman. Proverbs 7 tells the story of a young man who became involved with an impudent woman and the consequences of his actions.

People who dabble in Internet pornography and chat rooms that arouse their libido are not wise. Perverse talk and dirty jokes also hurt a person's ability to receive wisdom. Ephesians 5:3, 4 says, *"But fornication, and all uncleanness, or covetousness, let it not be once named among you, as becometh saints;* [4]*Neither filthiness, nor foolish talking, nor jesting, which are not convenient: but rather giving of thanks."* In the areas of sexual perversion, God is looking to see if you are wise enough to read His Bible, learn His opposition to such behaviors, and follow the Biblical exhortations addressing sexual sins.

9. The wise man is a learner. The wise man can learn by observing his world. Proverbs 6:6 says, *"Go to the ant, thou sluggard; consider her ways, and be wise."* The Bible says that we should consider the ant and learn the lesson of being industrious, economical, and filled with initiative. Nature is filled with Biblical truths. Consider how many times God mentions trees and fruit. Is there something to be learned about bearing spiritual fruit from the process by which a plant bears physical fruit? Is there a spiritual analogy between the growth of a tree and the growth of a Christian since Psalm 1 gives a promise that we can be like a planted tree?

Observation of nature is not the only consideration. Proverbs 21:11 says, *"When the scorner is punished, the simple is made wise: and when the wise is instructed, he receiveth knowledge."* Proverbs 27:12 says, *"A prudent man foreseeth the evil, and hideth himself; but the simple pass on, and are punished.* " The prudent man is the guide who makes wise the simple and is a wise man himself. This wise man sees evil and avoids it. He observes trouble and considers that he doesn't want to cross its path.

Proverbs 10:14 says, "*Wise men lay up knowledge: but the mouth of the foolish is near destruction.* " The wise man studies; he reads books; he did not stop learning in high school or college. The wise man chooses a hobby that enables him to learn. God sees the wise man desire to learn more, so God can trust this man by teaching him more about wisdom.

10. The wise man has a game plan. Proverbs 8:12 says, "*I wisdom dwell with prudence, and find out knowledge of witty inventions.* " *Prudence* in this verse means "leaving evil, walking away from it, and running from it." A prudent guide is a person who leads people away from sinful traps. As mentioned in the previous chapter, the counselor has a plan for the person seeking counsel to follow. The phrase "*...find out knowledge of witty inventions...* " speaks of a man who has a game plan and knows how to find a solution; this man is a problem solver.

Joseph, the son of Jacob, exemplified this type of wisdom. He displayed prudence when he fled from the seduction of Potiphar's wife. Because she lied and said that Joseph tried to seduce her, he was given the opportunity to show that he was a problem solver in prison. Genesis 39:21, 22 says, "*But the LORD was with Joseph, and shewed him mercy, and gave him favour in the sight of the keeper of the prison. 22And the keeper of the prison committed to Joseph's hand all the prisoners that were in the prison; and whatsoever they did there, he was the doer of it.* "

Joseph was a man of action; he was the doer; he had a game plan to accomplish something.

Genesis 40 tells the story of Joseph's interpreting the dreams for the baker and the butler. He saw that the two men were sorrowful and asked how he could help them; in essence, he was a counselor. Two years later Pharaoh had a troublesome dream, and the butler remembered how Joseph had interpreted his dream.

Upon recommendation by the butler, Joseph was brought before Pharaoh when the wise men and magicians could not interpret the ruler's dream. Giving credit to God, Joseph quickly interpreted the dream and provided a game plan. Joseph recommended four actions:

- Pharaoh was to select a wise and discreet man to govern the land.
- Pharaoh was to appoint officers who were under the new leader.
- The officers were to take up the fifth part of the land in the seven plenteous years.
- The food would be used to feed the people during the seven years of famine.

Pharaoh then said in Genesis 41:39, *"...there is none so discreet and wise as thou art,"* and made Joseph the ruler.

The worldly leader declared that Joseph was a wise man. The wisdom was evident because Joseph had a plan that came from God. He took God's plan and put it into action. God is looking to give His wisdom to the man who has a game plan. God will give wisdom to the man who looks at a tough problem, determines that he can figure it out with God's help, and then asks God for the wisdom to carry the plan through.

11. The wise man receives correction. Proverbs 9:8, 9 says, *"Reprove not a scorner, lest he hate thee: rebuke a wise man, and he will love thee. 9Give instruction to a wise man, and he will be yet wiser: teach a just man, and he will increase in learning."* A man who wants to receive wisdom to counsel must accept correction as a wise man would. The correct response to correction is to love the admonisher. The wise man will add the advice he has been given, correct his mistakes, and place the knowledge in his repertoire of counseling advice.

The natural reaction to correction is to make excuses and be defensive. Because of this, God says that no one should correct the scorner because he will only hate the one giving the advice more. A man's reaction to correction reveals if he is wise or scornful. God watches to see if a man will say and mean "It's my fault" or "I'm sorry" when corrected.

12. A wise man respects authorities. Proverbs 10:1 says, *"...A wise son maketh a glad father: but a foolish son is the heaviness of his mother."* A person who wants to obtain wisdom from God will please his "fathers." A previous point mentioned that a wise man has a good relationship with his father, but this point is different as it includes all God-given authorities. *Father* in the Bible sometimes refers to all of the elders and mature people who have taught and helped to rear a young person. Pleasing a leader requires wisdom. The individual who pleases his leader also pleases God because God knows that a man cannot please a God he cannot see if he does not please the authorities that he can see. A man rejects an increase in wisdom when he rejects leadership.

Twelve characteristics of wise men have been given. The counselor must be wise enough to add these characteristics to his life. This list is incomplete; Proverbs contains many more references on the subject of wisdom. Take the time to complete the following assignment and discover more about wisdom.

II Timothy 2:15 says, *"Study to shew thyself approved unto God, a workman that needeth not to be ashamed, rightly dividing the word of truth."* The exercises afford the opportunity to display wisdom to God by heeding His advice about studying and rightly dividing the Word of Truth.

CHAPTER FOUR

The Duties
of a Counselor

The first Biblical example of counseling was performed by God Himself. Adam and Eve were granted by God the choice of following God's will or their own will. God began to counsel this couple before they ever sinned, demonstrating that counsel is not limited to restoring the fallen. Adam and Eve left God's will when they sinned in the garden of Eden. However, God worked to bring them back into His will. God worked to help restore Adam and Eve. God helped Adam and Eve to recover themselves.

In order to build a Biblical model for counseling, this chapter is devoted to a Biblical examination of how God counseled this couple. As God counseled Adam and Eve, there are eight actions that He performed to help them recover themselves. These eight actions form the template that a counselor can follow to help the person seeking counsel recover himself.

The Counselor Defines. ——

A counselor defines what the one seeking counsel should become. A counselor is essentially a model. God modeled how to successfully live an eternal life in the garden of Eden. He put Adam and Eve in the garden where He walked. God gave them the chance to be close to Him. Parents model adulthood for their children. A pastor models an example for church growth. A coach models a pattern for victory. The counselor offers a mold into which a person may cast himself.

Counselors should allow people to be close to them in order to define what they are. If a counselor is a good Christian, he is a definition for being a good Christian. If a counselor and his spouse are good Christians and have a good marriage, then they define a good marriage. If the same couple has good Christian children in God's will, then they define a good Christian family. People who struggle need to be around other people who define.

A counselor should say, "Why don't you come see me?" This enables a person to see what the counselor is like. When a person says he needs help, the counselor should invite the person to spend time with him. A counselor's life must be worthy of imitating if he is to be a successful counselor.

A counselor defines purpose. God defined four purposes for Adam and Eve while they were in the garden of Eden:

- God told Adam to have dominion over all living things. (Genesis 1:26, 28)
- God told Adam and Eve to be fruitful and multiply and replenish the earth. (Genesis 1:28)

- God told Adam to dress and keep the garden. (Genesis 2:15)
- God told Adam not to eat the fruit on the tree of the knowledge of good and evil because His purpose was for Adam to be an everlasting creature. (Genesis 2:17)

A counselor is the pair of glasses that helps a person see a sharper, clearer image of his purpose. A counselor is like HDTV. Standard definition television has 480 horizontal lines on the screen while high definition television has 720 or 1,080 horizontal lines across the screen. These extra lines give a greater definition to the picture. The counselor is adding the extra lines of sound Biblical wisdom and practical advice to the picture that the person being counseled is seeing for his life. With these new items in life, the counselor helps a man see his potential or goal with a greater definition.

A counselor is like a fitness trainer who helps transform the flabby form into one that is muscularly defined. The person who seeks to be fit meets with a fitness trainer to learn how to train. The fitness trainer should define the model of fitness. He teaches a man how to do curls so that the man can develop his own biceps. The fitness trainer is defining for and teaching the man how to recover the form and muscular definition that was lost from his youth.

A counselor defines the known will of God for a man. God defined His will for Adam in the garden. There were many things Adam could do and only one thing that was disallowed. The known will of God is to walk with God. The counselor defines what it means to walk with God. He provides definitions for a person's role, prayer, soul winning, Bible reading, purity, responsibility, and work. When a man has communion with God, the unknown parts of God's will become defined for a man. When a man is near God, God will take the man where He is going. A counselor gives proven Biblical plans for how a man can recover himself. He defines limits and boundaries just as God warned Adam and Eve of their limits in the Garden of Eden.

A common root problem is that people do not know God's will for their roles. A husband might say that it is his duty to provide for his wife. A wife might respond that her husband's duty is to be someone with whom she could share her feelings. Neither is the complete Biblical model for a husband or wife. The example here shows that spouses both have several marital roles defined from the Bible.

The counselor does not define areas outside of the known will of God. No counselor should say, "I *know* what God wants you to do in life." The counselor should not play God because there is only one God. The counselor should not venture outside of his area to judge. This is a common temptation for counselors. When people struggle with sins, it is easy to preach a sermon on their sins. People who are seeking counsel do not need another sermon; they need someone to personally guide them through a plan for recovery.

The Counselor Provides. ——

A counselor provides resources and tools for a person to recover himself. Because God understood that it was not good for a man to be alone, He provided a help meet for Adam. God knew that in order for Adam to do His will, He needed to provide a helper. Adam looked through all of God's creation and found no suitable helper. God then gave Eve to Adam as his helper.

The counselor takes on the responsibility to outfit a person with the necessary resources. People seeking counsel need a curriculum from which to work, sermons to which they listen, targeted devotions from the Bible, and activities with other good Christian models. All of the resources should reinforce what the counselor defined.

The Counselor Allows Room to Grow. ——

A counselor allows the person seeking counsel to make his own choices. If that person is to recover himself, he has to be able to make spiritual decisions and apply Biblical truths in his own life. People often do wrong in groups but tend to do right by themselves. Since the person seeking counsel must learn to make his own decisions, a wise counselor allows him that right. The bottom line is that every man must learn to make wise choices.

Adam and Eve were allowed by God to make their own choices. He did not force Himself on them when they were tempted. He was not there to countermand the Devil's lies.

The Counselor Makes Himself Available. ——

After they sinned, Adam and Eve hid themselves when they heard the voice of God walking in the garden. God had not physically stopped them from sinning; He had not begged them to choose righteousness. Knowing that they had sinned and knowing where they were, He walked through the garden and said, *"...Where art thou?"* (Genesis 3:9) God was not accusing; He was not threatening. God was giving them an opportunity to meet with Him.

Likewise the counselor should make himself available to those seeking counsel. Counseling is nurturing and guiding someone so that he will be enticed to be where he should be. A strong relationship between a counselor and one he is counseling will entice that person to come back to get help.

The Counselor Questions and Corrects. ——

God corrected the situation in the garden by cursing the serpent and giving Adam and Eve clothing. Notice that God corrected by asking questions. God asked, *"...Who told thee that thou wast naked?"* and *"Hast thou eaten of the tree, whereof I commanded thee that thou shouldest not eat?"* (Genesis 3:11) When Adam answered that it was Eve's fault, God then asked her for her side of the story. He gave Adam and Eve an opportunity to confess their wrongdoing. Once they confessed, there was no need for a tirade because they had already admitted their need for correction.

The counselor often corrects by asking questions. Accusations and finger pointing do not solve a problem no matter how true they are. If a person is to recover himself, he must come to his own realization that he has done wrong and his own realization of the truth. Questions force a person to give an answer; they cause a person to face reality.

The Counselor Redefines. ——

In Genesis 3:16-19, God redefined Adam and Eve's life. After sinning, they were no longer allowed in the garden, so God described a new plan for their lives. He told Eve, *"...I will greatly multiply thy sorrow and thy conception; in sorrow thou shalt bring forth children; and thy desire shall be to thy husband, and he shall rule over thee."*

God told Adam, *"...Because thou hast hearkened unto the voice of thy wife, and hast eaten of the tree, of which I commanded thee, saying, Thou shalt not eat of it: cursed is the ground for thy sake; in sorrow shalt thou eat of it all the days of thy life;* [18]*Thorns also and thistles shall it bring forth to thee; and thou shalt eat the herb of the field;* [19]*In the sweat of thy face shalt thou eat bread, till thou return unto the ground; for out of it wast thou taken: for dust thou art, and unto dust shalt thou return."*

A counselor may have to redefine a course of action because someone has forfeited some rights. He might have to say, "You can no longer do that, but you should do this for right now." A counselor may have to redefine by showing the person who has sought counsel that he still possesses potential.

The Counselor Redeems. ——

Redemption is the process of restoring the dignity God originally gave to man. Genesis 3:21 says that God made a coat of skins and clothed Adam and Eve. The counselor draws a man back to where he should be. He gives a man opportunities for service. A counselor begins the process of reclaiming one's dignity.

The Counselor Redirects.

In Genesis 3:22-24, God took Adam and Eve out of the garden and put them into another place. When the person seeking counsel has lost privileges, the counselor shows him a new set of options. The counselor teaches him how to slowly rebuild his life. The counselor shows the person when it is time to temporarily step away from some duties to take the necessary time for healing, and he shows the person seeking counsel when it is time to resume those duties. The counselor helps direct choices for awhile. The counselor watches the person who has sought counsel blossom and mature. The counselor lets the person seeking counsel know when and what is open to Him.

These eight steps form an example of how God directed Adam and Eve's life. Accomplishing these eight steps may not happen in the same sequence, and many steps might have to be repeated as you patiently watch people fail and try again. As a counselor, you should pray for the wisdom to know when to apply each step and how to help those you are counseling complete each step.

Chapter Five

The Process
of Counseling

A t this writing, I have counseled for over 30 years, but I still refine my approaches to counseling as I learn to deal with people. My counseling failures sometimes came when I failed to apply Biblical principles or made myself the issue. Some of my failures were because of poor techniques in dealing with people. This chapter contains simple suggestions for counseling sessions that are based on my successes and failures.

1. Don't be proud. Seeking second opinions is not sinful and often proves to be very wise. A counselor must not be too proud to believe that only his advice can be obtained. If a couple chooses to consult another counselor, he should not take affront and think that they are spurning him.

When the Bible says there is safety in the multitude of counselors, it does not mean that a person should shop around for advice. Many people make the mistake of shopping around for the most palatable or tasteful suggestions. They will not get the help they sought because only the application of Biblical truths will solve their problem, and Biblical truths are not the most palatable solutions.

2. Listen to people. Experienced counselors can quickly diagnose problems, but they should still listen to those seeking counsel voice their concerns and hurts. If you do not listen, it is easy to jump to wrong conclusions. If you appear not to be listening, then people will not seek your help further because they think you do not care.

There is a minimum of two sides to every story, and some stories are exceedingly complex. No matter how much you trust someone, care about him, or believe him, there is another side to the story. A counselor cannot give advice before knowing all the facets of a conflict.

Remember that wisdom is seeing the big picture. You cannot see the big picture with—at most—half of the information. The wise person also holds the diagnosis in until afterward. The counselor should not speak or pass judgment immediately. Listening properly helps the counselor win the heart of the one seeking counsel, ensures that he has all the right information, and enables him to be a wise counselor.

3. Win the heart. A person's heart can be won by exhibiting grace and mercy. When the one seeking counsel has fallen, the grace that the counselor exhibits will win his heart. When the person seeking counsel thinks that no one will ever trust in him again, the counselor should be the person to help give him some self-worth. By listening instead of reacting, by offering hope instead of judgment, by giving encouragement and practical ideas, a counselor wins the heart.

Proverbs 11:30 says, *"The fruit of the righteous is a tree of life; and he that winneth souls is wise."* The verse does not exclusively refer to leading people to Christ; it is also talking about a person who can win the confidence of other people. The soul of man is that part which puts his confidence in someone. A soul winner doesn't win the body; he wins the soul or the confidence of a person. Likewise, a counselor has to win the confidence of other people.

4. Schedule an appointment for counseling. When an individual needs counseling, schedule a time to sit down and meet with him. Do not grant impromptu, spontaneous, or off-the-cuff counseling sessions because they are unrehearsed, and people are too valuable to rush. Impromptu counseling often leads to bad advice because the counselor sometimes speaks before he knows the full story. The counselor should be careful about giving advice when someone stops him to ask a quick question.

Proverbs 29:11 says, *"A fool uttereth all his mind: but a wise man keepeth it in till afterwards."* The wise counselor does not answer every question immediately. He sometimes has to take his time to pray and search the Bible for an answer.

Scheduling an appointment slows down the process, allows the person seeking counsel to make choices, and allows the counselor to gather more information. Quick and forced decisions are usually regretted decisions, so it is better to sit down, hear the entire story, and begin the process of recovery. By scheduling an appointment, enough time may pass to heal the problem. Time is one of the best healers of all wounds. What a person does with his time can allow him to react favorably to the hurts and the disappointments of life with a God-given resiliency. Therein comes healing.

Scheduling an appointment allows the person seeking counsel to deal with the problem a few more days. Many a person has come to an appointment and said, "We've already figured out our problem." Much of counseling is unnecessary because problems can often take care of themselves.

People might become offended when a counselor puts them off for a few hours or days or even weeks. When a person is offended, I tell him, "You are much too important, and this issue is too important for me to give you only a few minutes. Your life is much too valuable for something 'off-the-cuff.' Why don't you let me schedule a sufficient amount of time with you to treat this matter with the importance it deserves?" I make that statement because I truly believe that people are too important to rush, but I am also giving time a chance to work on them. If a person seeking counsel hears the Bible taught in church throughout the week, reads his Bible, or prays, God has an opportunity to counsel him. People who get back into their routines and allow time and distance to put the event into perspective will be much better served than if the counselor tries to handle the matter when emotions are hot and one's emotions are unbalanced. The counseling session will be more effective if the person seeking counsel has a calm perspective on his problem.

5. If possible, give advice that buys time. Giving advice that *buys* time relieves the tension and pressure to make an immediate decision. Many times in my counseling, I have been approached by a person who says, "I've been offered a promotion that involves a transfer. My boss says that I have to make my decision by tomorrow. What do you think?"

My answer to this man is, "Tell your boss that it is too important of a decision to make the choice right now. I don't believe God's will is decided under pressure. If they want you that badly, tell them that you need a few days or weeks to take your wife to visit the area. Look at churches, look at houses, and study your wife's countenance and spirit as you do it all. If it is a good decision, rarely will you have to be pressured to do it."

Pressure can destroy. People smoke their first cigarette because of peer pressure. People drink their first alcoholic drink because of peer pressure. Girls lose their purity because of pressure from a young man. Good counsel removes the pressure and allows God time to work on a person. Allow those seeking counsel to have the proper amount of time they need to make a decision.

6. Give options, not your opinion. What a counselor would do is unimportant; what God would do **is** important. When a counselor starts to say, "Let me tell you what I would do," he should shut his mouth. A wise counselor should be slow to give his opinion. A counselor would be safer saying, "I am not sure what I would do, but I will give you some options," or "Here are some things to think about in your situation." He should offer suggestions and actions to consider. Too often the counselor is trying to *cement* the person seeking his counsel to himself rather than strengthen his relationship with God.

A counselor can win a person's confidence by honestly saying, "I don't know." The person seeking counsel will know that he is not willing to risk steering him in the wrong direction. Thus, when the counselor does offer advice, it might be accepted by the one seeking counsel with the confidence that he is being steered in the right direction. When a counselor "does not know," he should recommend others who could help. Examples include doctors, attorneys, financial experts, and other professionals in the field of need.

Psalm 23:3 says, *"He restoreth my soul: he leadeth me in the paths of righteousness for his name's sake."* This verse clearly says that there is more than one path of righteousness. Thus, there is not one exclusive path to offer as a counselor. There is only one way to be saved, but there are many righteous paths, so give many options.

A counselor could read 50 books on marriage and glean from those books 50 good ideas on how to handle a marital problem. Since all of them are good ideas, he should offer the suggestions and let the person needing counsel choose which avenues he would like to try. The counselor should patiently wait to see how it bears out. If it fails, he can give him another option.

A counselor who only offers one path for a person to follow will be a disappointed counselor. Multiple pathways take pressure off everyone involved. Human nature causes a man to rebel when he is told he has to do something a certain way.

Offering only one option may well cause a counselor to lose his influence. A person seeks counseling because he lacks wisdom in an area and is not committed to doing right. Putting ultimatums on a person who is not doing right is senseless because he is not likely to follow the only path of righteousness.

7. Do not get emotionally involved. If you become angry at a person in counseling, you jeopardize your role as a leader and a guide. Perhaps you should recuse yourself and defer the counseling to someone else. Counselors must remain neutral, or they will be prone to giving poor advice.

8. Give the person seeking counsel something to do. People need more than words if they are to recover themselves; they need something to do. Recommend books that they can read or give them activity sheets to complete. Writing can be therapeutic because it affords people the opportunity to express their feelings. If a person can convey his feelings through the written word, it usually helps the recovery process. Counseling involves getting people to open up and talk a little bit, and writing on paper is a great therapy for people who are stressed and frustrated.

Many physical ailments are psychosomatic; these ailments have their roots in the stress, pressures, and emotional troubles that people have bottled up. The stress works its way out through a breakdown of health. People who are not emotionally and mentally healthy might have poor physical health. Writing is a powerful tool to help people cope with stress.

A 2005 report in the journal *Psychosomatic Medicine* concluded that patients with fibromyalgia reported less pain and fatigue over the short term after participating in writing exercises that described a traumatic event, described their feelings about the event, described how the event has affected their life, explained new insights they received from describing the event and what they could do differently in the future.[1] Similar benefits were found for reducing heart rate[2] and offering relief for patients who suffered with AIDS[3], asthma and rheumatoid arthritis.[4]

I always ask the person seeking counsel, "Do you read books?" If the individual replies that he does read books, I lend him a book and ask him to read it before the next time we meet. The plan that I give him is to read a chapter each night or even just one or two pages, but I stress that he should read a portion every day.

By giving someone a book to read, I am giving him a chance to see his problems in the text or be sparked by an idea that might open further dialogue with me. Remember that no counselor wants the person who has sought help to be dependent. Assignments give the person seeking counsel the opportunity to learn on his own and to recover himself.

9. Do not scold. Receive people with compassion rather than with condemnation. Bad counseling contains scolding; ultimately, it is ineffective. Scoldings frequently keep people from seeking help again. Scoldings convey an attitude of judgment and often prevent a counselor from being successful. Counselors should not jump to conclusions and then exhibit a tough attitude. In both II Samuel 22:36 and Psalm 18:35 the Bible says, *"...thy gentleness hath made me great."* Counselors must possess a gentleness that receives people just as Christ has received sinful men.

The Bible is strict enough; a counselor does not have to increase the rigidity of the situation. God is plenty tough on sin. A successful counselor is a human agency of understanding that allows the Word of God to scold and convict.

Many times a year people come to my office and say, "We have been coming to your church for six months, and we are very convicted because we are living together in fornication. The longer we go to Sunday school and hear your preaching, the worse we feel." Personally, I am thrilled when these couples come to me as their pastor.

At that point I don't say, "You better feel convicted! How come it took you a whole six months to reach that point? How come you didn't come under conviction when you started living together before you were married?" How unwise it would be to heap guilt on top of guilt!

At that point I do say, "I am glad you are coming faithfully to church."

They often ask, "What do you think about what we are doing?"

I do not say, "You're fornicators! God will judge you!"

Instead I say, "I think it is great that you came to see the pastor for advice. Let's talk about some options God has for you both." I avoid finger pointing when they are already pointing the finger at themselves. I want to lead this couple somewhere, so the last thing I am going to do is pummel them because they have been living in sin. The very fact that they are coming to my office proves they have the right attitude and have a sorrow for their sins.

The Bible says in Proverbs 9:8, *"Reprove not a scorner, lest he hate thee: rebuke a wise man, and he will love thee."* When a person comes to me for counseling, I don't know if that individual is a scorner or a wise man, so I don't risk scolding him. I will be tougher on a person the longer he comes to see me. Repeat sessions are a signal that the person seeking counsel believes the counselor; thus, the counselor can effectively tell him the truth in love. Also, the individual who is seeking a wise counselor is growing in wisdom and can probably handle some reproof.

The most difficult cases for a counselor occur when a person seeking help becomes belligerent. A counselor in this situation should say, "I am going to sit down and just show you what the Bible says. You can walk out of here upset, but your argument will be with the Word of God because I have no desire to squabble with you." Let the Bible do the scolding. I let the person know that I am humbled and honored to be his pastor and that my responsibility is to show him God's thoughts regarding the matter. Even sinners and belligerent Christians need a pastor who is patient and longsuffering with them.

10. Offer genuine praise. Proverbs 27:21 says, *"As the fining pot for silver, and the furnace for gold; so is a man to his praise."* A person is refined by genuine praise which should not be confused with flattery. Genuine, sincere, appropriate praise encourages people. A counselor does more by challenging a person with compliments than he does by scolding him with condemnation.

A counselor should give people hope and encouragement because the Bible offers hope and encouragement. Despite his situation, when the person being counseled leaves a counseling session, he should be able to say, "My counselor believes in me. I can do this." Counselors should give the people they are counseling the confidence to live another day. People will not find encouragement in their alcohol, their pornography, or their promiscuity. The counselor needs to be the man who frames a person's progress in a light that is praiseful. Counselors should compliment every bit of progress made by the one being counseled. A person is motivated to do more when he receives encouragement.

11. Ask people to write out their questions. Counselors should request that people write out their questions because it helps the person coming for counsel to understand what he desires to ask. Sometimes people cannot verbally phrase the problem; they know there is a problem, but they don't know how to express it. An unexpressed question leads to mental distress and frustration.

I usually ask people to write out their questions by our second meeting. On many occasions, those seeking counsel have returned to the meeting and told me that they no longer need to meet with me. They proceeded to share with me that once they wrote down the question, they knew the answer. That is an example of a person who recovered himself, and the goal of a counselor is to lead people to do just that.

12. Suggest older people who could help mentor the person seeking counsel. I Corinthians 11:1 says, *"Be ye follow-*

ers of me, even as I also am of Christ." Good counseling presents a good pattern, but every counselor is not always the right pattern. Counselors define, and the best definition might be someone else in the church. II Timothy 2:2 says, *"And the things that thou hast heard of me among many witnesses, the same commit thou to faithful men, who shall be able to teach others also."* Always be looking for and training others who can assist you in the counseling/mentoring process.

When the person seeking counsel is a woman, the counselor can direct her to an older married woman. Titus 2:3, 4 teach that the aged women should teach the younger women how to be women. A man who counsels a couple might not get through to the wife because she can build a wall of separation with the excuse, "You just don't know what it's like." As a man, I do not know what it's like to be a wife or a woman, so I can find a woman who can give her the sympathy she seeks while setting the Biblical model for being a wife.

Churches lose tremendous human resources when they ignore the older people who are no longer the "movers and shakers." These people may lack the steam, but they often possess the wisdom. The weakness of much counseling is the failure to offer a good pattern to follow. The resources of other mature people are so often wasted in a church.

13. Confront people's problems with God's truth. II Timothy 3:16, 17 says, *"All scripture is given by inspiration of God, and is profitable for doctrine, for reproof, for correction, for instruction in righteousness: 17That the man of God may be perfect, throughly furnished unto all good works."* Notice that the Word of God is profitable. Too often we put books written about the Word of God on a pedestal above the Bible. Not one book compares to the Bible.

People need to be reminded that their problem is a conflict with Biblical truth, not with humans or emotions or personalities. Some Christian counselors become excellent at handling people's problems and gravitate toward the use of psychology, logic, and smart talk, yet they never show the person who is seeking counsel what the Bible says. Books are good for illustrations, explanations, or assignments. Counseling should not be focused on what someone else said—unless it's God. I focus counseling on the Word of God. I essentially (but compassionately) say, "Read that verse. That is your problem."

A man's problem will never be fixed until he confronts the truth. The argument must be made from the Word of God. If the person asking for counsel argues, it should not be against the counselor's philosophy. His argument should be against the Bible. God can ultimately convict him; the counselor cannot.

[1]J.E. Broderick, D.U. Junghaenel, and J.E. Schwartz, "Written Emotional Expression Produces Health Benefits in Fibromyalgia Patients," Psychosomatic Medicine; 67:326-334 (2005).

[2] E.M. Epstein, D.M. Sloan, B.P. Marx, "Getting to the Heart of the Matter: Written Disclosure, Gender, and Heart Rate." *Psychosomatic Medicine*; 67:413-419 (2005).

[3] K.J. Petrie, I. Fontanilla, M.G. Thomas, R.J. Booth, J.W. Pennebaker, "Effect of Written Emotional Expression on Immune Function in Patients with Human Immunodeficiency Virus Infection: A Randomized Trial." *Psychosomatic Medicine*; 66: 272-275 (2004).

[4] J.M. Smyth, A.A.Stone, A. Hurewitz, et al. "Effects of Writing About Stressful Experiences on Symptom Reduction in Patients With Asthma or Rheumatoid Arthritis: A Randomized Trial." JAMA; 281(14): 1304-1309 (1999).

CHAPTER SIX

Psychological Problems

The Web site for the American Psychological Association defines *psychology* as "the scientific study of the behavior of individuals and their mental processes." *Psychology* is a Greek word that means "the word of the soul," or "the study of the soul." The counselor's job is to study the soul. Instead of looking at what modern psychologists say (though many have good information to offer), I will present the Biblical reasons that a person has a psychological (or soul) disorder and how to remedy these disorders. If a counselor knows why the person seeking counsel came for help, he can match the malady with a Biblical remedy.

Ignorance ——

Hosea 4:6a says, *"My people are destroyed for lack of knowledge."* A counselor teaches because people just aren't knowledgeable. Many problems could have been avoided if people had listened to their parents, Sunday school teachers, or pastor.

They did not listen carefully to what was being said, did not absorb the words, and did not retain the knowledge that was offered.

People miss knowledge when they sleep through church. They do not sleep because they are so busy and overworked; it is often because they do not eat well and do not have proper rest habits. Many problems could be solved by good health. Most people are ignorant about how the body works and unknowingly abuse it and justify the abuse by their schedule.

Most Christian people do not know what the Bible says about marriage, but they think they know all about marriage. Many people do not know the symbolism and beauty of marriage. Their image of marriage is no more mature than a seventh grader's view that it is all hugging and kissing. Sexual preoccupations in a marriage result from a lack of knowledge. The average boy is normal until puberty strikes between the ages of 11 through 13. During this time, someone gives that average boy some sexual knowledge. Unfortunately, he usually learns it in the back of the bus because his father doesn't discuss the matter. Dads generally do not discuss the subject because they were never properly trained and have lived inadequate sexual lives. The average husband brings to marriage bad habits and a pound of ignorance concerning intimacy, and ignorance and pride are poor ingredients for a healthy marriage.

When I first became a pastor, I performed the marriage ceremony for a couple who got a divorce within a few months. To prevent such a tragedy from happening again, I started a mandatory pre-marital class for anyone who wanted to get married in our church. The class teaches the couples their roles in marriage and potential areas for strife. None of the couples have been divorced since the class started. These couples are not being destroyed because of a lack or ignorance.

Counselors should look for the ignorance problem before they look for any other problem. Ignorance destroys because people become proud, ashamed to admit their lack of knowledge. As a result, complication has been added to complication, and many unhealthy situations are caused by ignorance problems. Ignorant people need a counselor to show them the truth.

Ignorance in the Scriptures also refers to one's ignoring what he does know. The counselor's duty is to teach, but also to reteach—to bring to remembrance what has been taught but ignored.

Bitterness ——

Hebrews 12:13-15 says, *"And make straight paths for your feet, lest that which is lame be turned out of the way; but let it rather be healed. ¹⁴Follow peace with all men, and holiness, without which no man shall see the Lord: ¹⁵Looking diligently lest any man fail of the grace of God; lest any root of bitterness springing up trouble you, and thereby many be defiled."* Bitterness is a common theme that runs through many people's problems. Bitterness is wrongly treated as a root cause when it is, in reality, a root symptom. The root cause for bitterness is failing of the grace of God.

What does it mean to fail at the grace of God? Hebrews 12 teaches that God sends negative circumstances and chastisement to perfect His children. If a person does not see the negative aspects of life as an act of grace from God, then he is failing at the grace of God. He then becomes angry with God, rejects Him, and judges Him as mean and unloving. The result is bitterness, a rejection of how God is trying to work in his life. A person essentially says, "God, if that is grace, then I don't want it."

Sometimes the most gracious thing God can do is hurt someone deeply because it gives access to His power. Paul said in Philippians 3:8-12, *"Yea doubtless, and I count all things but loss for the excellency of the knowledge of Christ Jesus my Lord: for whom I have suffered the loss of all things, and do count them but dung, that I may win Christ, ⁹And be found in him, not having mine own righteousness, which is of the law, but that which is through the faith of Christ, the righteousness which is of God by faith: ¹⁰That I may know him, and the power of his resurrection, and the fellowship of his sufferings, being made conformable unto his death; ¹¹If by any means I might attain unto the resurrection of the dead. ¹²Not as though I had already attained, either were already perfect: but I follow after, if that I may apprehend that for which also I am apprehended of Christ Jesus."* The Cross happened so that men might know Christ. Suffering comes so that men can better know God in life's ultimate relationship. Bitterness is an uglier end than accepting the sufferings from God because bitterness troubles, defiles, and causes fornication, profanity, and rejection.

Titus 2:11 says, *"For the grace of God that bringeth salvation hath appeared to all men."* If the grace that brought salvation was death on a cross, then why should anyone expect that the grace of God must always be a positive experience?

Disobedience ──────

Disobedience is "exalting one's opinion above God's Word"; it is not merely performing an action contrary to what is right. A disobedient person concludes that his way is better than God's way. For example, King Saul disobeyed when he battled the Amalekites. Samuel, the prophet and judge, received God's words and told them to Saul. Samuel told Saul that God wanted the Amalekites to be completely destroyed for their treatment of the Israelites in the wilderness. God specifically commanded that every man, woman, infant, child, and animal be destroyed. Saul destroyed all of the Amalekites except King Agag. Saul had the animals slaughtered except the best of the sheep, oxen, fatlings (animals fattened for slaughter), or lambs. Saul was disobedient because he handled the battle his way instead of God's way.

The first words out of Saul's mouth when Samuel arrived were, *"...I have performed the commandment of the LORD."* (I Samuel 15:13) Clearly Saul would not look at the truth because he did not follow the clear commands of God to kill everything.

Samuel confronted Saul by asking why he heard the bleating of sheep and the lowing of oxen. Saul denied that he was disobedient; instead, he shifted blame to the people. Samuel listed the ways that Saul was disobedient, so Saul then confessed his <u>disobedience</u>, but justified that he did so in order to sacrifice unto God.

Samuel famously answered, *"Hath the LORD as great delight in burnt offerings and sacrifices, as in obeying the voice of the*

LORD? *Behold, to obey is better than sacrifice, and to hearken than the fat of rams.* [23]*For rebellion is as the sin of witchcraft, and stubbornness is as iniquity and idolatry. Because thou hast rejected the word of the LORD, he hath also rejected thee from being king.*" (I Samuel 15:22, 23)

Grieved by this sentence from God, Saul gave another confession but blamed the problem on his people. Samuel told Saul that God would take the kingship and give it to another. After all of this, Saul still asked Samuel to give him honor.

Saul exalted his opinion above God's Word, and he went into a tailspin. He blamed his people, and then he blamed David. Saul consumed some of his later years hunting David. Whenever a person exalts his opinion above God's Word, he loses his moral direction.

Self-Righteousness ——

A self-righteous person will do right, but he will do it on his own terms. He is mistaken for being arrogant and cocky. Cain was self-righteous because he brought an offering to God that was not respected, and he became angry.

Genesis 4 records the story of Abel and Cain bringing an offering to God. In verse 4 the Bible says that Abel brought "*...of the firstlings of his flock and of the fat thereof.*" Abel brought the first and the best. This offering sounds similar to the requirements made in Leviticus 1:3 and 27:26. Leviticus 27 teaches that when a person tithes, he is to bring the firstfruits or firstling. Leviticus 1:3 teaches that an offering must be of the best possessions, and it is offered willingly. Abel brought the firstlings and the fat. *Fat* usually has a positive connotation when it is mentioned in the Bible because it refers to the best and the choicest.

Hebrews 11:4 says, *"By faith Abel offered unto God a more excellent sacrifice than Cain...."* The Bible says that Cain brought an offering, but it was not respected or not as excellent as Abel's. Bible scholars have hypothesized that Cain's offering may not have been acceptable because it was not a sacrificial animal, it was not the best, or it was not the firstfruits. For whatever reason, the offering was not acceptable. It is apparent that Abel knew what was righteous and obeyed, while Cain knew what was righteous but presented the offering that he wanted to present. Cain was self-righteous.

When I envision the story, I picture Cain laying good vegetables and fruits on the altar and Abel laying a fatted calf or lamb on the altar which he then killed. Fire came down and consumed the lamb as a statement of God's acceptance. Cain waited, but fire did not descend and consume his offering. Cain became angry with God. He brought an offering just as his brother had, but he did not bring an offering of which God approved. Cain wanted to offer an offering according to his way and not God's way.

Like Cain, many Christians within a church are self-righteous. They attend services and have some Biblical convictions if they are comfortable with them, but generally do whatever they want according to their own standards. They are insisting that God be content with what they offer.

Cain knew what he was supposed to do. He was supposed

to bring a calf or a lamb and sacrifice it. God would have burnt it with fire from Heaven in expression of his approval. Cain did not do anything wicked; he did not do what God required.

A counselor should probe the health of a person's walk with God because this will give him a clue if the person seeking his counsel is self-righteous. If someone is self-righteous, the conversation sounds like the following:

I might ask, "Do you read your Bible every day?"

The man replies, "I am a busy man, and I don't have a lot of time for that stuff."

"Do you attend the Wednesday night Bible study?"

He replies, "Brother Schaap, I work long hours and commute a long distance, and I don't get back until seven in the evening. God understands that I'm busy."

I will ask a few more questions like those and listen for the self-righteous answers. When I diagnose the problem as self-righteousness, I will respond, "It sounds to me like God just better understand who you are and the way it is going to be. You came to me for help, but you are telling me how it is going to be. Why did you come for help?"

Self-righteous people are looking for a magic trick to fix their problem. If the person seeking counsel will not address his self-righteousness, the counselor will waste his time because that person will not follow the Biblical plan presented by the counselor.

God is compassionate and patient with man. He told Cain that a sin offering was waiting by the door. If Cain would open the door, the lamb would jump into his arms. Cain could then give the proper sacrifice. Cain had to do the work, but he had to do it God's way. Cain refused because he was self-righteous.

Cain then murdered his brother, which proved that he had a psychological (soul) disorder. Cain killed his brother because he refused to submit to God's methods and wanted to kill the man who did follow God. People must be taught not to expect God to settle for what they offer and the way they offer it.

The Love of the World ——

If a person's struggle is the love of the world, the counselor must have a definition for the world. The Biblical definition is given in I John 2:15-17, which says, "*Love not the world, neither the things that are in the world. If any man love the world, the love of the Father is not in him.* 16*For all that is in the world, the lust of the flesh, and the lust of the eyes, and the pride of life, is not of the Father, but is of the world.* 17*And the world passeth away, and the lust thereof: but he that doeth the will of God abideth for ever.*"

The world is defined by three things: the lust of the flesh, the lust of the eyes, and the pride of life. Everything that is of the world can be distinguished by its association to lust or pride.

Lust is an out-of-control appetite, and pride is the arrogance that demands these appetites be filled. Instability occurs when the world develops appetites inside of a person that should not or cannot be filled. Pride makes a person ask why he can't have those things. Stability comes from a person's ability to say "no" to the world; otherwise, he is saying "yes" to the world and creating an appetite that breeds instability.

The love of the world is often introduced through success. Christians run into a trap because they quickly climb the corporate ladder due to their strong work ethic. As a person rises in position, his salary and demand for his work increases. As salaries rise, a person can buy more items that the world offers. Wealth satisfies appetites, but it also increases appetites. Wealth and possessions are not bad. The created need that you must have them is bad because it causes instability and psychological problems.

The couples who have marital problems due to the love of the world usually earn between $40,000 and $80,000. Very few married couples ask for counsel if their combined income is under $30,000. They have learned how to live on little due to hard work. The couple is so consumed with meeting needs and making it all work that they don't have time to fuss. If they do fuss, it does not last long because they are too tired or have to go to their second job. They find stability in a lower standard of living.

People who make $40,000 to $80,000 make more money than they need, but they aren't financially savvy enough to know how to use it. They frivolously spend money and then use their credit cards to live at a higher standard. They are usually good, generous people, but they spend too much of their money. This frivolous spending creates problems. They have a false illusion of how much money they have and soon realize the headaches and additional costs of spending lots of money.

Following After the Flesh Instead of the Spirit —

Romans 8:5, 6 says, *"For they that are after the flesh do mind the things of the flesh; but they that are after the Spirit the things of the Spirit. ⁶For to be carnally minded is death; but to be spiritually minded is life and peace."* Galatians 5:16 states, *"This I say then, Walk in the Spirit, and ye shall not fulfil the lust of the flesh."* The flesh and the Spirit war against each other. They each crave something.

Walking in the Spirit simply means that a person is in step with the Spirit. When a person walks with someone, he falls into step with the rhythm of the other. The Spirit takes people to a desired destination, so people should learn to be in step with Him.

A person does not walk in the Spirit when he is worldly and chasing fleshly appetites. A saved person is indwelt by the Holy Spirit Who wants to call the shots. A saved person also possesses a carnal nature that wants to call the shots. There is the rub. Which one will give in?

Galatians 5:26 explains that the person who is not in step with God is desirous of vainglory, provokes, and envies. *Vainglory* is self-centeredness or self-conceit; it means, "My way is right." Married couples not in step with the Spirit are constantly arguing over who is right.

Someone might ask, "Why can't they see it my way?" That statement is the flesh talking. Counselors should interpret this as a spiritual problem. Someone is not walking in the Spirit if he feels everyone has to see things his way. Another sign that someone is not walking in the Spirit is the fact that people aggravate him.

Have you ever noticed that God is unassuming? Only God deserves to have everyone see things His way. But does the Bible jump up and slap the face of those who do not read it? The Spirit of God does not coerce anyone to do His will. As powerful as God is, He does not push Himself on anyone. If God does not have to have His way in everyone's life, then couldn't a man also allow others not to see things his way?

Fear ———

Fear is a major determiner of actions. The National Institute of Mental Health says that anxiety disorders cause people "to be filled with fearfulness and uncertainty."[1] Approximately 40 million Americans are affected with anxiety disorders in a given year.[2] This number does not include people who have "relatively mild, brief anxiety caused by a stressful event (such as speaking in public or a first date)."[3]

The Israelites were afraid when they saw God's presence at the top of the Mount Sinai. In Exodus 20:19 they said to Moses, *"...Speak thou with us, and we will hear: but let not God speak with us, lest we die."* Moses responded in the next verse, *"...Fear not: for God is come to prove you, and that his fear may be before your faces, that ye sin not."* From the time of the exodus from Egypt in Exodus 12 and 13 through this incident in Exodus 20, the Israelites were characterized by fear. They feared when the Egyptians trapped them against the Red Sea, and they feared the lack of food or water.

People have natural fears and acquired fears. Acquired fears include fears of animals like mice or snakes, of heights, or of elevators. These fears are developed because people do not recon-cile perception with reality. Even though a person has a fear that is contrary to reality, a person will follow his perception before he follows the truth. Fear cripples. It is dangerous because it prevents people from dealing with their fears or their lack of perceiving reality.

A fear of authority figures could develop when a person is hurt or abused as a child or when he is mishandled by an authority figure. Many sinful lifestyles are a poor attempt to cope with fears formed from social issues, physical abuse, molestation, or hurts and pains that were not properly handled. A girl who lives with her boyfriend might choose that lifestyle to fill the void of an unfulfilled relationship with a father.

The Israelites had fears of uncertainty after 215 years of bondage. Freedom required them to take responsibility for themselves after receiving sustenance from the Egyptians. Imagine how afraid Americans would be if we suddenly lost our industrialization and modern conveniences to return to a life of agriculture. People would have fears about the source of their next meal and long-term provision. The Jewish slaves were probably told when to get up, when to go to work, when to eat, and when to go to bed. Although they were in bondage, they were secure in receiving food. Without that security, they developed fears. A generation of Jews never conquered their fears, and it cost them the Promised Land.

Counselors use the Scriptures to confront people's fears and show them the security that God offers. The Bible emphasizes that fear should not control a person. Fear is not conquered by repeatedly saying, "I will not fear! I will not fear!" It is conquered by taking inventory of fears, looking at Scriptural truths, and using faith to apply them.

Unbelief ——

The Bible teaches that one stage of faith is when a person is tempted to stop believing. Unbelief is not merely the absence of belief; that is non-belief. Unbelief is when a person had faith and then lost it. It is the same concept of tying and untying your shoes. You untie your shoes to undo what you had previously done.

Hebrews 3:12, 13 says, "*Take heed, brethren, lest there be in any of you an evil heart of unbelief, in departing from the living God.* ¹³*But exhort one another daily, while it is called To day; lest any of you be hardened through the deceitfulness of sin.*" This verse says that a person who has unbelief departed from God; thus, he must have been close to God at some point. Church rolls are filled with people who jumped into church, were excited about the things of God, and now no longer attend.

Spouses who feud sometimes say, "I used to love him, but I don't anymore. I once thought God could help our marriage, but I don't believe that anymore."

People are willfully and deliberately departing from God's plan. It is not God's plan for a couple to get divorced. If someone who stood with the Bible has marital problems, the only way he can reconcile his desire to divorce is by declaring that he no longer believes what he once believed. Unbelief is a mechanism that allows a person to avoid feeling he is a hypocrite.

Unbelief occurs when a person is hardened through the deceitfulness of sin. People fall for a lie that accommodates their new belief. They thought sin held a promise of fulfillment, but they were lied to by the sin. Unfortunately, they have not yet discovered the end of sin. This problem is common for people in their late teens and early twenties.

Sin deceives; it often looks good. Saved sinners will ultimately have to choose between their sin and their faith in God. Some people choose to drop their faith and disbelieve what they previously held true. Counseling people who have been hardened through the deceitfulness of sin is difficult because the deception has a seed of truth in it. Working with people who have turned their backs on God is not a matter of working with ignorance because they do have Bible knowledge; however, their knowledge has been perverted and twisted.

Curses ——

A curse is a generational sin or family sin that has not been Scripturally handled. God visits the iniquity of a generation three to four generations down the road. Curses are emotional and spiritual wounds inflicted in the formative years that were never balanced with Scripture, faith, and understanding.

Numbers 14:18 says, *"The LORD is longsuffering, and of great mercy, forgiving iniquity and transgression, and by no means clearing the guilty, visiting the iniquity of the fathers upon the children unto the third and fourth generation."* Iniquity is the internal permission that a person gives himself to sin. Iniquity is not the sin; it is what tells you that it's acceptable to sin, that it won't hurt you, and why you are allowed to sin. People depart from the faith because sin's deception leads to a mental or physical sin. Iniquity is what justified the sin.

God told the Israelites that whatever sins they justified would hinder and plague three or four successive generations. God did not make those generations sin, and He did not give them reason to sin. He watched for a generation that would put away those sins and redeem the next generations.

The Israelites were filled with unbelief and did not enter the Promised Land. The generation led by Joshua then faced the same trials of having faith in God, but they were serious about conquering these problems. They succeeded in knocking down the walls of Jericho and possessed the Promised Land. They broke the curse.

For many years, I ran a church bus route in East Chicago that brought people to church. Many children would come, but their parents often refused to attend when I invited them. The children loved riding the bus and attending church, but as the years rolled on, their attendance decreased. Ten years later, those children were pregnant teenagers. By the time those church bus kids turned 21, they wanted their children to ride my bus. I would invite those new parents, but they would refuse to attend. That second generation fell for the same deception of sin as their parents. One generation later, they were in the same situation as their parents and hoping that the third generation would come to church on the bus. The iniquity was visited upon them, but they didn't correct it. Do you think that third generation is more likely to grow up in the church or to commit the sins of the parents? God is looking for a generational warrior to break the curse.

I wonder how many people are alcoholics who did not have to succumb to the temptation had their grandfather dealt with the sin properly. I wonder how many ruined lives marred by fornication could have been avoided had a mom or dad dealt with the problem. People struggle with psychological problems because the sins of the past were not confronted.

Habitual sins that cannot be overcome clue me in to a curse. As a counselor, I often say, "I want to know about your mom and dad. I want to know about your grandpa and grandma. What kind of man was your grandpa? Tell me about your grandma; what kind of woman was she? Tell me how your grandparents treated your mom and dad." Spousal abuse is a common generational problem. Child molestation tends to run in families. In my counseling of pedophiles, I do not recall meeting one who had not had someone violate him when he was a young boy, and it was often a family member. Instead of dealing with his problem, he indulged.

Failure in Stewardship ——

Malachi 3:7-12 mentions a curse due to a failure in stewardship. Many people do not realize that they are not owners, but stewards of God's possessions. Christians don't own anything. Psalm 24:1 teaches that everything is on loan from God. *"The earth is the LORD'S, and the fulness thereof; the world, and they that dwell therein."* Christians don't even own themselves because I Corinthians 6:20 says, *"For ye are bought with a price: therefore glorify God in your body, and in your spirit, which are God's."*

Psalm 8:6 teaches that God gives man dominion over the earth, but God is still the owner. Possessions only belong to a person to the extent that God allows one to tend to His things. I'm not a liberal environmentalist, but I believe that we should take care of the earth and not pollute because the earth is the Lord's.

God allows men to abuse His possessions to a point. Every man has a free will, but at some point, a man will face the consequences of his irresponsibility. Poor stewards abuse the privilege of being the caretaker of God's body, God's health, God's property, God's money, God's buildings, and God's earth. Poor stewardship causes psychological problems due to arrogance, pride, stupidity, foolishness, and bad behavior.

An Unscheduled Life

King David fell in trouble when he was unscheduled. II Samuel 11:1 says, *"And it came to pass, after the year was expired, at the time when kings go forth to battle, that David sent Joab, and his servants with him, and all Israel; and they destroyed the children of Ammon, and besieged Rabbah. But David tarried still at Jerusalem."* David should have been going to war; it was the appointment he should have kept. Instead, he stayed home, lounged around, and started looking for something to do. David spotted Bathsheba bathing on her roof, committed adultery with her, impregnated her, and killed her husband to cover up the pregnancy. David had a sordid mess to sort out because of his fornication. The psychological problems that followed were a result of an unscheduled life.

Psychological and emotional problems can stem from not following your schedule. A disciplined life is exceedingly important. Dr. Jack Hyles, my predecessor, believed the undisciplined life was the primary cause of all problems. If one could discipline one's schedule and live by the schedule, many problems would be solved. If a person would get up at the same time, go to bed at the same time, eat each meal at the same time, and go to work at the same time, he would lead a more balanced and orderly life.

Demons and Spirits ——

Jesus dealt with amazing problems in the New Testament that were demonic in nature. These problems still exist, but they are now labeled with medical names that classify them as diseases and might not be treatable with medicine.

Luke 8 tells the story of the demoniac of Gadara. When Jesus entered this city, he was met by a naked man who lived among the tombs. The Bible says that the devil drove him into the wilderness. Men of the city had tried to chain the maniac, but he broke the shackles. The maniac cried and howled all day and night and cut himself with stones. The man was possessed with many demons and spirits which Jesus expelled.

Our world wants to call alcoholism an addiction; perhaps there is a reason that alcohol was commonly known as "spirits." People have pornography problems—an addiction to looking at people wearing no clothes. This maniac had no clothes on, and he was possessed with devils. Demons and spirits are behind pornography because they lead to nakedness and debauchery. I believe that someday we will discover that the pornography industry is filled with devils and demons and spirits that have disguised themselves into bodies after which men and women lusted.

Alcohol and pornography destroy families because they introduce demons into the home. Alcohol is not just a liquid, and pornography is not just a picture. They are doorways that introduce the power of Satan into the home. The Bible says that alcohol introduces foolishness into a life; it deceives, and whoever is deceived thereby is not wise.

The Bible describes people who take drugs as sorcerers or as people involved in witchcraft. *Sorceries* and *witchcraft* are translated from the Greek word *pharmakeia* which is the source of the English word *pharmaceuticals*. Witchcraft is found to be a common addiction in the end days when God destroys the world. The Bible teaches that men are so committed to their pornography and their drugs that God will allow visible devils to torment them.

Revelation speaks of music that worships devils. Worship and praise go hand in hand. When Christians worship God, they often sing songs. When people worship devils, they play anthems and sing to these devils. Today we see this in gothic music, rock music, and other worldly music. Our church is adamant about not letting certain types of music into our church. We do not want to open a doorway allowing the wrong spiritual influences.

Alcohol, pornography, drugs, and certain kinds of music are an entrance into a devil's world, putting the user in touch with demonism. People who meddle with these portals open doors to unclean spirits. When counseling, I will probe into a person's music and his usage of alcohol, drugs, and pornography. My goal is remove Satan's influence from people's lives. Sex, drugs, and rock music aren't the ultimate issue. The issue is the effects brought about by those behaviors.

The word *music* comes from the word *muse* which means "to think and meditate." The Bible says that we gain success and prosper by meditating on its words. A person who listens to rock music meditates, thinks, or muses as he is mentally transported into another world. Music can be an addiction because it delivers an individual from the world he does not like into a world in which he can dream and fantasize. A person literally opens a door into another world, but he does not realize that it is a world of demonic influence.

Remorse and Regret ——

Matthew 27 tells the story of Judas' betraying Jesus. Verses 3 and 4 say, "*Then Judas, which had betrayed him, when he saw that he was condemned, repented himself, and brought again the thirty pieces of silver to the chief priests and elders, Saying, I have sinned in that I have betrayed the innocent blood. And they said, What is that to us? see thou to that.*" Judas then hanged himself.

Thousands of teenagers attempt suicide every year over remorse and regret. The largest reason teens attempt suicide is because a love relationship was broken. The remorse and regret over the death of a relationship creates psychological problems for anyone of any age.

Prematurely Obtaining One's Desires ——

II Samuel 13 tells the story of Amnon and his half sister Tamar, the object of desire. Amnon wanted to marry her. There is nothing wrong with getting married, and in that time it was permissible to marry one's half sister who was born of a different mother.

Instead of properly obtaining her hand in marriage, Amnon listened to Jonadab, his friend and cousin. Jonadab coached Amnon to feign sickness and ask King David if Tamar could come and bake something for him. Once Tamar was alone in Amnon's quarters, he was to grab her and rape her.

Amnon followed the plan. Tamar begged and pleaded that he not do such a thing. She said that David would definitely give her as a wife if he asked. She wasn't opposed to marrying Amnon, but she wanted to follow the proper procedures at the proper time. Amnon wanted her immediately and had his way with her. After consummating his indulgent lust, he told Tamar to get out of his life.

Tamar was devastated and said that sending her away was worse than the rape. He should have at least married her and fulfilled his duty of caring for her. Amnon called his servants and commanded that she be taken from his sight. Tamar was emotionally crippled because of this tragedy.

Amnon's psychological change was caused by prematurely obtaining that which was lawful to have. Undesirable repercussions are caused when people pursue their desires before they have the character to manage them. People who marry too soon have such problems. A child who is promoted too quickly through school and doesn't socially assimilate may have these problems.

Besetting Sins and Weights ——

Hebrews 12:1, 2 says, *"Wherefore seeing we also are compassed about with so great a cloud of witnesses, let us lay aside every weight, and the sin which doth so easily beset us, and let us run with patience the race that is set before us, ²Looking unto Jesus the author and finisher of our faith; who for the joy that was set before him endured the cross, despising the shame, and is set down at the right hand of the throne of God."* A besetting sin or weight is the sin, habit, or hobby to which a person turns when he feels pressured, distressed, selfish, angry, or bitter. When a person feels that he cannot cope with life or he is overly fatigued, he is a candidate to indulge in besetting sins or weights.

People who don't want to give up their stature or position find a besetting sin in which they can indulge. Adults have turned to the same besetting sins since they were teenagers or younger. It is a habitual door that they have locked but to which they still possess the key.

Besetting sins can be caused by temper. When people are stressed, I ask them, "What is it you turn to?" I ask that because they will continue to turn to that for relief. It might become an addiction.

The 15 problems discussed in this chapter survey Biblical examples of psychological problems. A counselor must have the wisdom to discern which of these problems a person has. Once he deduces the problem, he must continue to aid the person by giving him a Biblical plan for defeating the problem.

[1]"Anxiety Disorders," NIH Publication No. 06-3879.

[2]R.C. Kessler, W.T. Chiu, O. Demler, and E.E. Walters, "Prevalence, Severity, and Comorbidity of Twelve-Month DSM-IV Disorders in the National Comorbidity Survey Replication (NCS-R). Archives of General Psychiatry. 2005; 62(6):617-627.

[3]"Anxiety Disorders," NIH Publication No. 06-3879.

CHAPTER SEVEN

Gauging the Results

What will you expect to see in the life of a person who has sought your counsel? How do you know when progress is being made? As a counselor, it is important to gauge the effectiveness of your counseling. The best Biblical example of a person who recovered himself is the prodigal son. This chapter briefly looks at the signs that demonstrated he had recovered himself. They are the following:

1. Personal accountability
2. Confession of sin against Heaven and then against man
3. Demonstration of genuine humility

The prodigal asked his father for his inheritance, received it, and then left home. He wasted his money with riotous living, and then a famine struck the land. The prodigal fed swine for a citizen of that country. Starved, the prodigal desired to eat the husks that he fed to the swine.

Luke 15:17 continues the story, *"And **when he came to**

himself, he said, How many hired servants of my father's have bread enough and to spare, and I perish with hunger!" No one will come to the Father unless he first comes to himself. The prodigal took personal accountability. He realized that his problems were his fault.

Personal accountability is a sign of growth because there will be no change until a person says to himself, "I got myself into this situation, and it is my responsibility to do what is necessary to get myself out." No one will recover until he comes to his senses and takes personal responsibility. The problem might be physical, financial, moral, or other. Regardless of how the person seeking counsel entered the storm, he must take personal responsibility and steer himself out. Even if the fault does not lie with the person seeking counsel, he may have to assume responsibility to fix the problem.

Calamities, or so-called "acts of God," are some of the hardest storms for someone to take personal accountability because there is no immediate cause-and-effect connection. If a marriage is in financial trouble, the married couple can point to the debt they accrued. If a marriage is in moral trouble, either the husband or the wife can point to the affair he/she had. If a marriage is troubled by a disease, rarely is there fault that either spouse can assume. The victim still has to assume the personal responsibility of doing what it takes to see if the disease can be treated. If someone was molested or abused, he or she has to take responsibility and say, "This is my problem; I will deal with it. I won't run."

Joseph of the Old Testament had to come to himself when

he was in the pit, when he was sold to Potiphar, when he was placed in prison, and when he had to serve the Pharaoh. These calamities and struggles were not his fault, and some were brought on because of righteousness.

A counselor cannot make anyone else personally accountable. A person recovers himself; thus, he must come to that conclusion by himself. The prodigal took personal accountability which started his path to self-recovery.

After coming to himself, the prodigal said in Luke 15:18, *"I will arise and go to my father, and will say unto him, Father, I have sinned against heaven, and before thee."* The second tell-tale sign of growth is the realization that a sin is primarily against Heaven.

If the person seeking counsel is the sinner, then he must realize that he sinned against Heaven. If he was the victim of a sinner, then he must realize that the ultimate problem was not the sin against his body, but the sin against Heaven. No one will receive help if he views the problem on a horizontal plane with humans. If the vertical connection with God is not straight, no horizontal relationships will be reconciled.

When I counsel a couple who are struggling with an adultery situation, I look at the spouse who did not commit the sin and say, "May I remind you that you did not write the Ten Commandments. You do not have a personal law that says to your spouse, 'Thou shalt not commit adultery.' The vows that you repeated were given to you by a pastor who included fidelity in the vows to remind you that the relationship is forged in Heaven before it is forged on earth. You did not write the rules; God did, so the sin is primarily against God."

If the person seeking counsel is an offender, the counselor should ask questions that provoke the one seeking counsel to ask himself, "Have I sinned against God?" People who have done wrong like to point fingers at how everyone else is treating them. When I hear those phrases, I ask, "What are you missing?" or "What is it you are not getting?"

If someone answers, "I should have been smarter and not gotten caught," then he is not realizing that he has sinned against Heaven.

The prodigal son hit the nail on the head when he confessed that he had sinned against God. Once he realized that his problem was with God, it was easier to fix the horizontal relationships. The prodigal then said to his father, "I have sinned against you." Human relationships will heal when the relationship with God is healed.

Counselors cannot reconcile the person seeking counsel with God. The counselor helps the Spirit make inroads that will lead a man to say, "What did I do? I was wrong. God, I'm sorry."

The third sign of growth was displayed in verse 19 when the prodigal said, *"And am no more worthy to be called thy son: make me as one of thy hired servants."* He displayed genuine humility and repentance. The counselor can see genuine humility and repentance when the one seeking counsel looks to redeem the relationship he destroyed.

The prodigal didn't declare himself to be worthless. He said that he was not worthy to be the son, but he was worthy to prove that he could be his father's best servant.

The wrong attitude wallows in self-pity and pride. It says, "I messed up, but I can't go back to church because no one will forgive me and nobody cares about me." Such people think that they are the issue, and humility knows that the individual is not the issue.

The counselor's job is to help a person redeem himself through work. A person is making inroads when he wants to come to church and sit there without having a position. He is humbling himself when he asks, "May I serve in the church? May I work on a bus route? May I greet at the doors? Is there any way that I may contribute?" These questions show that a person is not worried about losing face or returning to a position. The person is more interested in finding his self-respect and worth.

If a person won't work to earn his self-worth, the counselor can't make him feel worthy. The counselor can say, "I believe in you. I am pulling for you," and pump up his spirit, but he cannot restore dignity.

As the person who has sought counseling progresses, the counselor should look for three signs that the individual he has counseled is recovering himself. Each admission is a step toward recovery. The wise counselor will ask the questions that provoke a person to consider whether or not he is taking personal accountability, seeing that his sin is foremost against Heaven, and demonstrating genuine humility.

CHAPTER EIGHT

Danger Signs in the Counseled One's Life

I Timothy 1:19 says that some people have shipwrecked their faith. Counselors are needed to discern the danger signs of pending shipwrecks. We call it backsliding, and an able counselor will aid a person in righting the ship before it crashes. People will wait too long to get help, so a good counselor will discern the warning signs, discern what type of help a person needs, and offer it to that person.

People who disappear from church often did not seek counseling. Pride makes many people gamble with their future because they won't seek help at signs of trouble. In the counselor's office, many people will say through their tears, "Where did we go wrong?" Men and women have said, "I didn't realize my marriage was in this much trouble," when they received divorce papers because their pride prevented them from recognizing and admitting to their problems.

Preventive maintenance is ultimately a lot cheaper than

breakdown maintenance for a vehicle, and it is always less stressful. It is better to fix your brakes before they fail than to fix them after they have failed and caused an accident. Parents must learn to deal with discipline problems soon after the incident. Parents should learn to discipline their children at early ages so the child's life doesn't disintegrate in the teenage years. It is more "economical" to deal with a four-year-old's tantrum in Wal-Mart than it is to deal with a pregnant teenager. For couples, it is more economical to pay for a couples' retreat than for divorce fees and alimony.

This chapter is devoted to recognizing the signs of backsliding. These danger signs are extracted from the story of Cain and Abel. Most Christians will not realize they are backsliding, so the counselor must learn to recognize the signs and speak the truth in love to those who are seeking his counsel.

Feeling Disrespected and Mistreated ——

Genesis 4:3-5 says, *"And in process of time it came to pass, that Cain brought of the fruit of the ground an offering unto the LORD. ⁴And Abel, he also brought of the firstlings of his flock and of the fat thereof. And the LORD had respect unto Abel and to his offering: ⁵But unto Cain and to his offering he had not respect. And Cain was very wroth, and his countenance fell."*

Cain and Abel both brought an offering to the Lord. God respected Abel's offering, but He did not respect Cain's offering. God's response to the two offerings was obvious. God sent fire down to consume the animal sacrifice of Abel but did not consume Cain's vegetable offering that was laid on the altar.

Cain was angry over this rejection; perhaps he felt disrespected and mistreated.

If Cain and Abel had a counselor or mentor, Adam was it. Adam knew what Cain felt, for he had also been harshly rebuked by God when he was expelled from the Garden of Eden. Adam could have taught Cain how to respond properly.

A wise counselor needs to learn when and how to assert himself. Cain needed a guide to say, "I've been through this, and let me tell you how I handled it." Adam either was unaware of what was happening or he chose not to get involved in the hurt feelings of his son.

A Fallen Countenance ———

God asked Cain in Genesis 4:6, "...*Why art thou wroth? and why is thy countenance fallen?*" The countenance is the expression on someone's face; it is how a person looks at someone. When Cain felt rejected, his countenance was depressed or sad.

A fallen countenance is a withdrawal of emotion and a pulling away from authority. Teenagers will naturally draw away from their parents for the sake of identity and independence, but they should never pull their heart away from their parents. When teenagers gravitate to a pastor or youth pastor, a parent might be jealous, but this could also be a natural pulling away because the teen is still in contact with authority. Pulling away from authority is not okay when it is a departure from all authority. A person who pulls away from his authorities is exhibiting a danger sign that he will soon backslide.

The first telltale sign that someone is pulling away from me is that he will not look at me when I am talking to him in the office or during a sermon. I gauge people by observing physical and emotional withdrawals. When a person changes how he thinks about someone, his countenance will also change. Observing if someone treats you well or poorly is not self-serving, selfish or judgmental.

Paul said, "...*Demas hath forsaken me....*" (II Timothy 4:10) He didn't say, "Demas hath forsaken God," or "Demas hath forsaken the faith." It was personal. Demas left Paul's work, and Paul knew something was wrong because Demas forsook him.

Counselors should never judge someone's countenance based on one encounter. A person might be having a bad day, not feeling well, have gotten scolded, or had their finger slammed in a door. He should wait a week or two before deciphering a person's countenance. I check up on people when I have seen a fallen countenance and emotional withdrawal for a few weeks.

Counselors must have their antenna up; they need to receive signals. They must keep their ears and eyes open for changes in attitude and behavior toward authority, toward church, and toward God. Backsliding people leave fingerprints and DNA samples everywhere. The counselor has to be like the forensic scientist who finds the clues and solves the crime.

A Critical Attitude About the Righteous ——

Abel was the righteous kid who was in step with his authority. Cain was the kid who hated the righteous kid because of his own lack of righteousness. Cain's critical attitude is obvious from Genesis 4:8, 9, which says, *"And Cain talked with Abel his brother: and it came to pass, when they were in the field, that Cain rose up against Abel his brother, and slew him.* ⁹*And the LORD said unto Cain, Where is Abel thy brother? And he said, I know not: Am I my brother's keeper?"* Cain slew Abel because *"...his own works were evil, and his brother's righteous."* (I John 3:12) Cain's ultimate criticism of Abel was demonstrated with murder. Such physical attacks are thankfully less frequent amongst Christian brothers in a church, but the verbal attacks are filled with a wrath equal to Cain's.

The book of James describes the tongue as a fire, a defiler of the entire body, an arsonist that sets on fire the course of nature, untamable, an unruly evil, and full of deadly poison. (James 3:5-8) Jesus taught in the Sermon on the Mount that a person who called his brother a fool was worthy of hell. (Matthew 5:22) The tongue is a weapon that can be used for good and evil. The backslider dices authorities and friends with his tongue. Paul warned Timothy of vain jangling and babblers. (I Timothy 1:6; 6:20; II Timothy 2:16) *Jangling* and *babbling* are words for idle talk that has no purpose. People who speak idly are exhibiting warning signs of backsliding.

Counselors should listen to how people talk about each other and keep their ears open for the tongue that criticizes righteousness. They should listen for husbands and wives who speak ill of each other. They should tune in to teenagers speaking critically of parents and authorities. They should listen for people who badmouth the powers and positions that God has ordained. When a counselor hears critical talk, he ought to ask,

"Is there a problem? Do you want to talk about it?"

The telltale sign of a bad marriage is that someone will bad-mouth their spouse to other people. Faithful are the wounds of friends, and a counselor has to be enough of a friend to say, "I'm listening to you talk, and I think you have some issues that need to be dealt with. I am worried about you." Counselors do not listen in order to report on the rotten state of someone's life; they lovingly insert themselves in an attempt to help people to recover themselves.

Counselors must have the gumption to call people on the carpet from time to time. When people are too timid to intervene, they watch people turn upside down and fall out of church. Counselors must speak the truth in love to salvage people.

A Rejection of Responsibility ——

God asked Cain, *"...Where is Abel thy brother?"*

Cain responded, *"...I know not: Am I my brother's keeper?"*

God then confronted Cain when He said, *"...What hast thou done? the voice of thy brother's blood crieth unto me from the ground."* God passed a sentence on Cain when He said, *"And now art thou cursed from the earth, which hath opened her mouth to receive thy brother's blood from thy hand; 12 When thou tillest the ground, it shall not henceforth yield unto thee her strength; a fugitive and a vagabond shalt thou be in the earth."* (Genesis 4:11, 12)

Cain was fully deserving of this punishment. He had committed the crime and was fortunate that God had not sentenced him to immediate death. Cain once again rejected his responsibility and was filled with self-pity when he claimed, "...*My pun-ishment is greater than I can bear."*

A counselor will know a person is backsliding when he hears:

- "Don't blame me!"
- "Why are you always picking on me?"
- "Why do you think I'm always doing something wrong?"
- "Everybody is mistreating me!"
- "Do you know how bad I've got it?"
- "I can't believe that he has it in for me."

When I was an administrator at Hyles-Anderson College, I would contact students who did not return from the previous year. One year I called a young man named John who had been in my classes. I said, "Hey, John, this is Brother Schaap."

John said, "Wow, Brother Schaap, you called me on the phone?"

"Yep. I called because your carcass isn't here at college," I teasingly said. "I miss you. Why aren't you here, buddy?"

His tone changed when he said, "I'm just not coming to school."

"I'm sorry. What is wrong? It sounds like you are a little bitter about something."

"Well, I have a right to be bitter."

"If you tell me about it, I can help you."

"You can't help me."

"I bet I can. Just tell me about it. If I can't help you, I will say 'good-bye', and you won't come to college. If I can help you, it might change your life."

John thought about my proposition and said, "All right. Last year something terrible happened, and I got demerits I didn't deserve."

I said, "Man, I hate that. What a bummer. I have been there before."

John told me a story of how he received 25 demerits. He appealed to a staff member at the college who told him, "Sorry, that is just the way it is going to be. You are going to get the demerits."

I said, "Don't you just hate that when that happens?"

John said, "I hate it, and I'm not coming back to school."

"What if I got those demerits off for you?"

He said, "You could do that?"

"Absolutely. I have the power to take off demerits. I will go to your records as soon as I get off the phone and remove the demerits."

"What's the catch?"

"Just one. I will remove all of the demerits that you didn't deserve if you allow me to give you demerits for every offense you committed that wasn't caught."

John asked, "Is it too late to register?"

John returned to school because I noticed that he wasn't in his usual place and sought him out. When I spoke with him, I noticed that he was rejecting his responsibilities to be accountable for his actions. I heard him say that he wasn't being treated fairly. John wanted to come back to school, which is why he quickly recovered himself. I showed him the folly of his logic, and he conceded that his logic was flawed.

Counselors must look for the warning signs. People who have a chip on their shoulder or who drop out of life need someone to interpret their backsliding signals. A counselor needs to discern when a fallen person needs a friend.

By the time Cain uttered his excuses to God, he had already been sentenced. A good counselor will see these warning signs and intervene before a person ruins his life. Cain literally went to hell. What if Adam had intervened when Cain was wroth? What if Adam had said, "Cain, I've been scolded by God too. Let me tell you how I dealt with it. God told me that I had to work hard, so I went and tilled the ground." Perhaps Cain could have been restored with graceful intervention.

CHAPTER NINE

Mistakes Counselors Make

ounselors fail to help people when they reinforce negative concepts in those whom they counsel and condemn the future generations to repeat the same errors. Bad decisions in people's lives are often the product of a reaction to or emulation of a poor model set by a counselor or mentor. The books of I and II Samuel, I and II Kings, and I and II Chronicles contain portraits of poor counselors, written for our examples as we counsel and mentor.

The lives of Eli and Samuel are depicted in the early chapters of I Samuel. Eli, the priest, reared Samuel. He was a fairly good priest because he was diligent and was personally concerned about his priestly responsibilities. When the ark was taken by the Philistines, Eli died because he felt a personal responsibility for the ark. Despite these good traits, Eli was a horrible counselor and mentor for his two sons, Hophni and Phinehas. They were morally impure, perverted and wicked. The Bible describes them as sons of Belial, which means they were good for nothing. God said that Eli failed to restrain his sons; he did not discipline his boys and allowed them to continue in their office despite their vileness. God killed Eli's sons in battle and held Eli accountable for these judgments.

In spite of his failure with his own sons, Eli trained Samuel to be an outstanding priest and prophet. Samuel caught Eli's professionalism, but he also caught his mentor's child-rearing skills. Samuel's boys were judges in Beersheba who sought lucre, took bribes, and perverted judgment. The Israelites rejected Samuel's sons from being judges over them. They wanted a king like the other nations had, and they were given Saul as a king.

Saul's early days were filled with righteousness and mercy. King Saul took responsibility for David when he would no longer allow David to go back home after the defeat of Goliath. Saul was essentially saying, "I am responsible for you," and he became David's mentor and counselor. David became subject to the strengths and weaknesses of Saul. Unfortunately, this coincided with Saul's becoming delusional and paranoid. Saul tried to kill his own son, Jonathan, and David. The epitome of poor counseling might be an attempt to kill the one being counseled.

David, a man after God's heart, grew up to be a tremendous warrior and leader. However, there were some equally tremendous failures in David's life when it came to his role as a mentor. At 17, David defeated Goliath and gained enough respect to lead an army. As an older man, David could not lead his own home, did not properly rear his sons, and faced tragedy because of his children. Amnon raped his half-sister and was killed by his brother Absalom, who had all of the talent and character to be king. David then survived a coup led by Absalom, who was murdered by David's general of the army, Joab.

If you had to choose a mentor and a counselor from among two priests or two kings all chosen by God, none of the choices would seem bad. Yet each of these men had failures in counseling and mentorship. Counselors fail when they react to issues without dealing with the issues that are pertinent to a developing and moldable person. Each generation then repeats the same mistakes which develop into societal problems. This chapter is devoted to examining six significant mistakes that Saul made as he took responsibility for David. His mistakes are admonitions for every counselor.

1. Saul's baggage from his own problems created conflict. Saul failed a test God gave him. Saul was instructed to kill King Agag, all of the Amalekites, and all of the livestock. Saul did not completely obey the command and was thoroughly chastised by Samuel who said, *"...thou hast rejected the word of the LORD, and the LORD hath rejected thee from being king over Israel...*[28] *The LORD hath rent the kingdom of Israel from thee this day, and hath given it to a neighbour of thine, that is better than thou."* (I Samuel 15:26, 28)

From that day forward, the forefront thought in Saul's mind was, "Who is going to replace me?" He must have often wondered who was this man who was better than he.

After David defeated Goliath and the Israelites slaughtered the Philistines, Saul would not let David return home. As they returned from the battle, the women sang, *"...Saul hath slain his thousands, and David his ten thousands."* (I Samuel 18:7)

The Bible says that Saul was angry and displeased. In a jealous anger, he said, "...*They have ascribed unto David ten thousands, and to me they have ascribed but thousands: and what can he have more but the kingdom?*" (I Samuel 18:8) Saul suspiciously kept his eye on David from that day forward. In his heart, he probably thought, "So this is the guy who is going to steal my kingdom!" Saul eventually tried to kill David in a desperate attempt to preserve his kingdom.

Saul missed the opportunity to play a crucial role as David's counselor. Knowing that he was going to be replaced, he could have contributed to the future kingdom and trained his successor. He instead fought his successor.

This is a common problem in father-son relationships; dads fight against their sons. Fathers fight their children when they try to live vicariously through their offspring. Kids get turned off to the direction in which Dad is pushing. Sons can feel that they are not allowed to develop into manhood when Dad is trying to manipulate the future.

This is a common problem with in-laws. Strife occurs when a future father-in-law exercises grotesque manipulation of his daughter and future son-in-law for the sake of assuring himself that he still has power. Dads look silly when they take one last dying gasp of manhood to prove that they have enough testosterone flowing through their systems. Mothers-in-law can perform the same manipulation on a son's wife because they can't stand the thought of losing their little boy.

People must face the reality that the end of their kingdom will come. Parents need counseling because they are not prepared to be separated from their children. The counselor has to remind parents that their power will end in that relationship. The counselor will someday be replaced by a younger man. They should let their successors inherit a wonderful kingdom.

Speaking humanly, part of my success as pastor is due to my predecessor, Dr. Jack Hyles, who realized that his kingdom was coming to an end and prepared our church for a successor. He and I were together on a preaching engagement when he mentioned to a pastor that our church should build a 7,500-seat auditorium.

The pastor said, "Brother Hyles, why don't you build it?"

Brother Hyles replied, "Because I don't think it is fair to the guy who is coming after me to have to pay the bill that I create." As his successor, I'm glad he felt that way. As the current pastor, I would hate to die and leave the building debt that I created to another man. By the time I retire, I want our church to be debt free. I want my successor to be able to spend more money than I did on remodeling buildings and winning the lost to Christ.

Counselors must be careful not to become grumpy and irritated. Saul did because he was hurt by the mistakes of his past. He forfeited his opportunities when he could have held the throne longer and passed it on successfully. Saul chose to hurt David instead of edifying him. Saul should have said, "Samuel prophesied you will be the next king. I am proud of you. Let me teach you what I have learned. Let me put my soul into you. Let me teach you some wisdom." Saul was jealous and envious instead.

2. Saul was so fixated on his present problems that he had a bad spirit. Saul was troubled by an evil spirit as he considered his problems. Consideration of the text leads me to believe that Saul was moody; he went through cycles of depressions. Today we would call him a manic-depressive or bipolar. Throughout his relationship with David, Saul repeated the cycle of loving David and then hating him. Again the Bible exemplifies that Saul's problems led to the hurt of his follower David.

Marriages can become contentious. Husband and wife continue to run on six cylinders when the other two cylinders are broken. Cranky people fixate on their problems and forget their responsibilities. Spouses nursing a bad spirit forget that they have to rear the kids. They get irritable with the neighbor, and the issue brews and stews inside of them. A person with a problem at work couples it with an unhappy marriage; failure to deal with these issues can lead to a mental or physical affair that pacifies the sorrow. A spouse can easily lose track of the young man and young woman whom God has ordained him to raise; instead, the spouse seeks his escape world.

When a counselor focuses on his problems, he fails. A person who focuses on the problems is not focused on finding a solution. A lack of solutions means that someone will get hurt. David had a spear thrown at him because Saul couldn't deal with his emotional problems. Counselors must learn to deal with their current problems before dealing with the problems of others.

3. Saul had an unforgiving and unrepentant spirit toward Samuel. Saul felt injured by Samuel because the prophet delivered the news that God would take the kingdom from him. Saul's hurt was unfounded because Samuel was merely God's messenger; yet Samuel was the focus of Saul's anger. Saul harbored bitterness, and David suffered. Saul sought for a place to lay the blame.

Followers of unrepentant mentors and counselors don't have javelin holes in their skin; they have javelin holes in their soul. Bitter parents have left our churches because they would not forgive another member. I wish that it worked, but it doesn't. Look at their children 20 years down the road, and you will find adults who are barely in church, barely understand the Bible, and are paralyzed in the maturation process because they were never taught how to handle a problem in life without harboring bitterness.

Bitter pastors lose their church members. Bitter leaders are quickly exposed to their followers as out of control and incapable. Bitter people have not dealt with a heart issue that is an unrepentant attitude and an unforgiving spirit toward someone. Bitterness always hurts the one who is bitter and his followers instead of the object of the bitterness. The counselor must remove the root of bitterness from his life.

4. Saul was critical of Jonathan, another mentor in David's life. The Bible does not give Jonathan's age, but I assume he was older than David. Jonathan, Saul's son, was exceedingly capable to lead armies; he had the tools to be a king. Jonathan knew that he would not inherit the throne and that David would be the king. Jonathan decided that he would teach David how to be a king. David received Jonathan's robe, which was a symbol of Jonathan's succession to the throne. Jonathan gave David his sword and other symbols of his authority. Jonathan was a tremendous example as a mentor because he stripped himself of his power and bestowed it upon his protégé.

Saul displayed horrible skills as a mentor when he became critical of Jonathan. I Samuel 20:30-34 says, *"Then Saul's anger was kindled against Jonathan, and he said unto him, Thou son of the perverse rebellious woman, do not I know that thou hast chosen the son of Jesse to thine own confusion, and unto the confusion of thy mother's nakedness?* 31*For as long as the son of Jesse liveth upon the ground, thou shalt not be established, nor thy kingdom. Wherefore now send and fetch him unto me, for he shall surely die.* 32*And Jonathan answered Saul his father, and said unto him, Wherefore shall he be slain? what hath he done?* 33*And Saul cast a javelin at him to smite him: whereby Jonathan knew that it was determined of his father to slay David.* 34*So Jonathan arose from the table in fierce anger, and did eat no meat the second day of the month: for he was grieved for David, because his father had done him shame."* Saul was angered because he knew that Jonathan was in David's corner.

Counselors should not criticize other mentors in the life of the one seeking counsel. It is harmful for a counselor to criticize a husband to a wife and belittle his authority in the home. Criticism of a parent to a child lessens the God-ordained authority in the eyes of the child. The counselor may not think that another is qualified to win the heart of the one seeking counsel, but criticism of the other mentor hurts the individual being counseled. He sees two adults fighting against each other.

5. Saul displayed a controlling and manipulating attitude. Chapter 21 of I Samuel tells the story of David's receiving Goliath's sword and the shewbread from Ahimelech. When Saul heard of Ahimelech's deeds, he lost his dignity and said, "*That all of you have conspired against me, and there is none that sheweth me that my son hath made a league with the son of Jesse, and there is none of you that is sorry for me....*" Saul became pathetic. He murdered Ahimelech because he worried that this high priest had conspired against him.

Counselors and mentors control and manipulate when they believe the issues are about them instead of the people they were called to help. Parents who have counseled and mentored their children to adulthood may attempt to control and manipulate as they see their children preparing for marriage or leaving home.

6. Saul did not create a safe zone for David. David had a second chance to kill Saul, but he refused to harm the Lord's anointed. When David called out to Saul instead of killing him, Saul said in I Samuel 26:21, "*...I have sinned: return....*" Saul wanted David to return to the palace—the very place where Saul had previously tried to pin David to the wall with a spear.

Instead of choosing the palace, David chose to live among the Philistines, the sworn enemies of God and the native people of Goliath. David felt safer with his nation's enemies than with his king in his previous position. What kind of a mentor is a father or mother when their child would rather go to the dangers of the world than to go home?

Counselors and mentors need to have a safe zone for those under their care. It's like a game of tag where there is a home base where one is always safe. People need a counselor and mentor with whom they feel safe and secure. If they don't feel safe, they won't open up and trust the counselor.

The sum of these mistakes is that a counselor cannot be worried about his own feelings. When someone cannot objectively view a situation, he will be a poor counselor. Saul lost lots of opportunity for influence because he could not balance his emotions with his duty to serve others.

CHAPTER TEN

When the One Being Counseled Fails

The Apostle Paul speaks as a brokenhearted man in II Timothy 4. He is hours away from exiting this world and entering Heaven as he writes to Timothy, a younger man in his forties who is the pastor of a large church in Ephesus. Paul's broken heart is not due to his impending beheading; it is due to the failures of his followers. He said, *"For Demas hath forsaken me, having loved this present world, and is departed unto Thessalonica; Crescens to Galatia, Titus unto Dalmatia. ¹¹Only Luke is with me. Take Mark, and bring him with thee: for he is profitable to me for the ministry."* In the same epistle Paul said, *"...all they which are in Asia be turned away from me...."* (II Timothy 1:15) Paul was ready to die, but he was saddened that his followers had turned their backs on him. Some quit and bailed out; others were in the ministry but preached against Paul.

Every mentor and counselor will become disappointed in

his followers. Some followers will quit; some will betray the counselor. During my 30-plus years in the ministry, I have been saddened by the choices of many followers. People might receive Biblical counseling for four to six sessions and then drop out. I have been ignored and disrespected by people whom I have helped. As a counselor, I find it frustrating to invest time in teaching people Biblical principles that are rejected so quickly. On extremely frustrating days, I have fantasized about packing up my Bible and running to a mountain retreat.

Quitting because others fail is not an option. II Timothy takes away my excuses. Paul said that he fought a good fight; he said that he kept the faith; he said that the reward is laid up for him in Heaven because God knew his works. As I look to the Bible for encouragement, I know that I can also look to the Bible for help on how to react when followers fail.

This chapter is devoted to seven Biblical examples of good things to copy and bad things to avoid when followers fail.

1. Counselors should not fight a follower's desire for independence. The parable of the prodigal son exemplifies how the father did not fight his son's independence. Luke 15:11-12 says, "*...A certain man had two sons: 12And the younger of them said to his father, Father, give me the portion of goods that falleth to me. And he divided unto them his living.*" The beginning of this story is filled with heartbreak but turns into sweet redemption. The Bible does not record an altercation. The Bible does not record a struggle over the boy's request. The parable states that the father "*—divided unto them his living,*" or, restated, that he honored his son's request. The prodigal might have returned because his father did not fight his desire for independence.

The people who have followed you will need to express their independence, even though they may not choose to express it in a holy manner. Personally, it is hard to let go of someone into whom you have invested your life; but realistically, you wanted the same independence when you were growing up. This tug of war is wrought between parents and teenage children who are considering their college and career options.

When someone fights the desire for independence, he drives the follower further away. The wrong reaction is to "put your foot down" or butt heads. The right reaction is to work with his desires so the counselor doesn't lose his influence. If the issue becomes the counselor's will against the will of the one being counseled, the younger buck is going to win. He will prove his ability to win by walking out, showing he can be his own man, and ultimately, hurting the counselor.

2. Counselors should not get into a control battle with their followers. The father did not have a control battle with his prodigal son. He knew that his son would express his independence and that he could only lose the control battle. Bosses should not get into these struggles with employees; pastors should not get into these struggles with a church. Pastors have asked me, "How can I keep this family at my church? They've been here a long time, and now they are leaving."

I reply, "Tell them your heart and how you feel. Write them a nice letter. Tell them you love them. If they want to leave, give them a pleasant farewell. Don't fight their decision."

Brother Hyles often said, "I keep my people on the open market." That sounds good from the lips of a pastor, but it's harder for a parent to say to his child. Parents cannot control children as they get older, and a common parenting problem that counselors see is a parent who won't allow his child to make choices once the child is old enough to be making his own decisions. People should not get into control battles because they don't run anyone's life except their own. The same issue is reversed later in life when adult children want to control their senior citizen parents.

Parents need to be taught to direct their child's life when he is small. The parents make all the decisions when the child is younger; but as the child starts maturing, there should be more and more decisions that the child is allowed to make.

3. Counselors should not promote failing followers in the hope of gaining their loyalty. Eli's sons, Hophni and Phinehas, were called the sons of Belial and labeled as people who did not know the Lord. Despite their obvious failures, Eli gave each the position of priest. God was angry with Eli and said, *"Wherefore kick ye at my sacrifice and at mine offering, which I have commanded in my habitation; and honourest thy sons above me, to make yourselves fat with the chiefest of all the offerings of Israel my people?"* (I Samuel 2:29) God later said in verse 30, *"...for them that honour me I will honour, and they that despise me shall be lightly esteemed."* God was telling Eli that he should only promote people to a position of honor if they had first honored God.

I have talked to many pastors who told me of offering a

new position as an employee or Sunday school teacher to a man who was planning to leave his church. The result was a problem that had escalated. As their followers failed, they in turn failed to follow the Biblical principle of only honoring people who were honoring God. I know parents who have ruined their businesses because they offered a wayward son a partnership when they saw he was straying from the Lord.

Counselors should not promote people whom they influence unless the people have bought deeply into their vision. Otherwise, it might ruin the counselor's work. When I make a careful and critical examination of a potential employee, I am looking for the person who has been loyal to the church program and displayed exemplary character without getting a paycheck. No one should be promoted to a visible, public position in order to secure his or her character.

4. Counselors should not ignore the failure. If a follower is not toeing the line, the counselor should face the issue directly. He should ask the follower where he wants to go and what type of person he wants to be. Sometimes followers need a point-blank, face-to-face, honest and simple chat. When they go astray, they need someone to speak the truth in love.

Eli ignored the problems. Inherent in the promotion of his sons was ignoring their sins. He swept the problems under the rug and lost his life and heritage for it. The Bible says to turn the other cheek, but that does not refer to turning your head to look the other way when someone does wrong. The expression of independence can be accompanied by an attitude. Counselors and mentors should not fight feelings; they should fight actions.

5. Counselors should not give up on followers before God gives up on the followers. Samson had the greatest potential of any of the judges. He was a young man with great power and great potential; he was a young man upon whom the Spirit of the Lord rested. Samson performed great feats, but he had a soft spot in his head and heart for unholy women. His lust cost him his power, his prestige, his ministry, his eyesight, and ultimately his life. He became enslaved to the Philistines. Many would cast Samson as the poster child for failed followers, but the Bible tells a different story.

The final chapter has not been written about followers. The final chapter was written for Samson, and Judges 16 records that, "...*Samson called unto the LORD, and said, O Lord GOD, remember me, I pray thee, and strengthen me, I pray thee, only this once, O God, that I may be at once avenged of the Philistines for my two eyes. 29And Samson took hold of the two middle pillars upon which the house stood, and on which it was borne up, of the one with his right hand, and of the other with his left. 30And Samson said, Let me die with the Philistines. And he bowed himself with all his might; and the house fell upon the lords, and upon all the people that were therein. So the dead which he slew at his death were more than they which he slew in his life.*" Samson's life would have been an extremely sad story if it had ended with his grinding at the mill like an ox, with his eyes out and his head bald. However, the Bible says that "...*the hair of his head began to grow....*" (Judges 16:22) God gave Samson one final chance in which he accomplished more than he had in the entirety of his previous years.

Followers such as students or children might break hearts by playing the fool and choosing an ungodly life. The counselor needs to remember that the final chapter has not been written. Many followers realize in later years that they have played the fool. They might not be the pastor or missionary or deacon that someone dreamed they would be, but they might have some potential and energy to give to the Lord.

Don't give up hope on people. A 30-year-old is still considered young. He still has more than half of his life to live. Some people do not turn around and show contrition for their foolish years until their forties or fifties or sixties. God's purposes may not include the counselor's seeing the finished product, so he should not give up on people.

6. As long as the follower is not hurting the team, keep him on the team. Jesus didn't give Judas the boot when He knew that Judas would betray Him. Jesus said, "*...Have not I chosen you twelve, and one of you is a devil?*" (John 6:70) The very next verse says that he was speaking of Judas Iscariot.

Judas wasn't hurting the team. At the Last Supper, the night Jesus was betrayed, Jesus said, "One of you is going to betray me." Counselors should not go on witch hunts. Jesus could have gone on a witch hunt, but instead He washed Judas' feet hours before the betrayal. Judas was treated with mercy and grace.

The disciples all said, "Is it I?" None of them said, "I know it's Judas." None of the other disciples suspected Judas. They were able to minister to people's needs while carrying a failing follower.

I have had more than one pastor call me and say, "I have someone on my staff who is two-faced. He acts one way in front of me and acts another way behind my back. I want to fire that stinker as fast as I can."

I ask, "Is he hurting anyone in the church?"

I often hear the pastor's reply, "He's not hurting anyone that I know of. Everyone seems to think he is wonderful."

If they say that, I reply, "You will hurt yourself if you fire him. Even if you are right, you will hurt yourself because all the people would have to find out all the details you know, and that would be scandalous. Is he shaming the cause and name of Christ? Is he in adultery or drinking?"

"He's not doing anything like that. He is just two-faced."

I say, "Just keep him on your staff. Keep him on your team because Jesus kept Judas on the team."

Leaders must ask themselves, "How much can I put up with when it is stuff that only I know?" Judas wasn't committing adultery; he wasn't getting drunk. He was stealing the money, but only Jesus knew that. He hid behind the excuse, "I'm using it for the poor." [Note to pastors: Staff members and deacons who steal money need to be confronted and most probably dismissed.]

People seeking counsel should be kept close to the counselor's side because they need their mentor. Judas needed Jesus, and Jesus kept him around since he wasn't hurting the cause. The failing follower needs to still be in the choir or in the youth group or teaching a Sunday school class as long as he isn't bringing anyone down with him.

7. Counselors should not lose their focus when the person seeking counsel loses his. Leviticus 10 tells a somewhat unfamiliar Bible story of Aaron's sons, Nadab and Abihu. These two boys were burnt to death when they offered "strange fire" before the Lord. In the previous chapter, God had told them the specific requirements for the burnt offerings.

My opinion is that part of the problem was that the boys were drunk, because in verse 9 Moses told Aaron that the new rule would be to not drink wine or strong drink when they went into the tabernacle. I also believe that they had taken the fire from the wrong source, and they performed the act with drunkenness and with levity.

Aaron was devastated by the loss of his two boys. The entire process in the tabernacle was new to him, so he had to learn a lot of instructions for the different offerings that must be presented. When his boys were killed, Moses told Aaron to keep working and instructed other family members to remove the bodies. Aaron was not allowed to grieve at that moment, nor was he allowed to rend his garments—the cultural expression of grief—because they were the priest's clothes.

Moses was saying that the people would grieve for Aaron. Moses gave more instructions, and Aaron essentially said, "Can you lighten up a little bit? I'm distressed, and I can't keep all of these rules straight." Moses told Aaron to take off the priest's garments and take the rest of the day off.

Counselors cannot lose their focus when their followers lose their focus. This is a sensitive topic because no one wants to be callous toward those who are grieving. I have often heard an injured spouse or parent or family member say that he cannot go on because his loved one faltered. But people have to go on in their grief. God wants people to let others grieve so that they can find comfort in the love of others. That's what a church is for; the church is vital to allowing people to cope with grief.

People who are grieving over the choices of a follower need to keep putting one foot in front of the other. Brother Hyles said that the grieving person needs to get up, bathe, get dressed, eat, get in the car, and go to work. He needs to do the same on the following day because it helps to keep his focus.

Counselors cannot let the grief of a foolish follower take away their faith in a fabulous Father. They must have faith in God. When the counselor's heart is broken, he must remember that his faith is in God and not in the loved one.

Moses might come across as heartless for telling Aaron to keep working, but he knew that the nation was watching. If the counselor falls apart, all of his followers will see it. The one who broke the counselor's heart will have a greater reason to doubt God because his mentor cannot hold himself together. People need their counselors to hold it together because their reaction is great evidence of God in Heaven.

8. Counselors should not let the failures of followers keep them from other good Christians. Paul and Barnabas had a dispute over John Mark in Acts 15. Paul and Barnabas were returning to the cities where they had already preached. Barnabas wanted to take his nephew, John Mark, but Paul did not want to take John Mark because earlier he had deserted them. Paul and Barnabas went their separate ways because to Barnabas the blood family was thicker than the spiritual family. Barnabas did not properly deal with the failure of his nephew because it resulted in keeping him from the great work he had established with Paul. Later in life, Paul recommended that Timothy work with John Mark who had become profitable. Barnabas was never heard from again. John Mark was reconciled to the work, but Barnabas was not.

Many leaders are so embarrassed by the failures of their followers that they cut ties with the family of God. Parents who are embarrassed by their children's actions drop out of church because of the shame. People deal with their hurt feelings by walking out on God, but they compound the problem.

The counselor should be as the prodigal's father who stayed where he was and had an open door to which his son could return. The prodigal knew where to go because his father didn't change. Counselors must stay in church and stay in their ministry when followers fail because followers need a place to which they can return.

With death impending, Paul wrote that he had fought the good fight. Asia had turned against him, and he didn't know who was on his side. He had invested his life in so many, but they had bailed out on him. Paul was content that God knew what he had accomplished. As Paul did, so must the counselor fight the good fight, finish the course, and keep the faith. When followers fail, the counselor must keep walking his course because someone else needs to see him walking it.

CHAPTER ELEVEN

Before You Start to Counsel

Jesus Christ is the ultimate counselor and mentor. *Counseller* is a name ascribed to Him in Isaiah 9:6. He was an advisor to His disciples and to the crowds who thronged Him. A great display of Christ's readiness to counsel took place when the Pharisees confronted Him with the woman taken in the act of adultery. John 8 records that in the midst of Jesus' teaching the people in the temple, the Pharisees interrupted His teaching by setting the woman in His midst.

As a pastor, I don't like when people leave during my sermon because it interrupts my train of thought and catches the attention of my church members. Jesus had it worse because the Pharisees interrupted His teaching and challenged Him. Jesus' situation brings up questions that each person must answer if he desires to be a counselor.

1. **Are you willing to be confronted with the hurts and failures of others?** Jesus was faced with a case of adultery, a

crime punishable by death in His days, and a "big" sin—as some people call it—in our modern days. Are you willing to work with the mess that people make of their lives? Could you compassionately handle the lasciviousness of the adulteress and the hostility of the Pharisees? Can you look as Jesus did on the woman and have mercy without judgment?

2. Are you willing to have interference in your own purposes and plans? Counselors receive calls at all hours of the day and night. People in need of help will show up at the counselor's office or at his door and expect the counselor to drop what he is doing. Counselors have to shove their plans to the side and shelve their schedule to accommodate others. The price of making a difference in people's lives is the interference from the complications they have created. Jesus might have had a great sermon planned that day, but it was interrupted by the accusations of the Pharisees.

Those complications cause counselors to be sidetracked from their tasks, but they must not become sensitive and say, "Why are you bothering me?" People do not interfere with the job of a counselor; people are their job. When people have an emergency, they aren't going to care that the counselor has paperwork to do. They care that he embraces trying to solve their problem. People who have their eyes fixated on their problems will not notice the inconvenience they create for the counselor. When someone has to have his problem solved, the counselor must say, "I'd be happy to help. That is exactly what I want to do right now." If you can't say and do that, you should not consider being a Biblical mentor.

Sin and sinners take center stage. The Pharisees placed the adulteress "in the midst" of the action. Sin has a way of taking over the headlines and the attention. Counselors must be prepared to be confronted with sinners.

3. Are you able to respond gently to the accused and the accuser? The Pharisees accused the lady when they said, *"...Master, this woman was taken in adultery, in the very act. 5Now Moses in the law commanded us, that such should be stoned: but what sayest thou? 6This they said, tempting him, that they might have to accuse him."* (John 8:4-6) How would you respond to the trap that the Pharisees were trying to set for Jesus?

How will you respond when the self-righteous people condemn another? Will you maintain the same gentle spirit when speaking to the accusers and the violators as you do for the victims? Can you act the same toward those who condemn as you do toward those who are caught in their sin? Most people would rebuke the Pharisees who were interrupting and berate the lady who was the adulteress, but a mentor cannot have that attitude.

The Bible says that *"...the servant of the Lord must not strive; but be gentle unto all men, apt to teach, patient, 25In meekness instructing those that oppose themselves...."* (II Timothy 2:24, 25) The gentleness must extend to all men. Can you handle people without blowing up in their face? The counselor must handle the sin and the sinner without being self-righteous. Could you be gentle with a child molester? That's a tough demand, but the Bible says that the servant of the Lord is *"...gentle unto all men...."*

4. Can you defend being merciful without violating your integrity? Jesus did not condone the woman's actions, but He displayed a way to be merciful without breaking the law. He said, *"...He that is without sin among you, let him first cast a stone at her."* (John 8:7) Jesus gave grace without throwing out the Word of God.

Christian schools are usually filled with rules. Administrators are often asked by parents to make exceptions to the policies. The administrator would love to say, "This is the rule. We don't break rules—end of discussion."

The counselor finds a way to give people what they want without violating the rules. The counselor will not break the law nor break policy, but will find a way to give grace without voiding the rulebook. You can't bypass the truth in order to accomplish righteousness because truth is the pathway of righteousness. If you can't figure out a path of grace that doesn't tread over an established system of law, don't be a mentor. Too many people would sell the truth to be kind. Others would rather destroy mercy to preserve the law. Can you fulfill the law without destroying it?

In Matthew 5:17, Jesus said, *"Think not that I am come not to destroy the law,...I am not come to destroy, but to fulfil."* Yet, He was unrivaled in His compassion. Fulfilling the law was tougher and more demanding than anyone thought, but Christ was more merciful than anyone else. Counselors don't have to choose between mercy and righteousness; they can give both. If they can't, they are not thinking very hard. The letter of the law kills; it is not the counselor's duty to kill someone by using the law. Counselors find a way to help a person within the context of the law. They must find a way to use the rules to teach a person about grace and mercy.

If the law isn't there to help people, then you don't understand the law very well. If you break the law and say, "People are more important than rules," then you are a liar. You are not helping that person; you are hurting that person's integrity, and you are pulling down what you stand for in the system. People see you as someone who provides the easy way out.

Don't hide behind rules in order to insult, hurt, or dismiss someone. Discipline should provide people with a new respect for the law, and the disciplined should find honor in the way they were handled.

5. Can you humble yourself when everyone around you is exalting his sin or self-righteousness? Jesus stooped down and wrote on the ground when He was confronted. As the Pharisees raged, Jesus symbolically humbled Himself by bending down. A mentor must be able to sit down when everyone else is standing up in a rage. A mentor brings peace when others have brought chaos. A mentor brings a fire hose when others are pouring on gasoline.

I have had counseling sessions where adults who had been sitting around the table were suddenly standing and yelling. Standing is an action that conveys someone is ready to take action. People stand during a counseling session when they are angry. I have never seen two people physically fight in my office—and I have seen people fight in my office—who did not first begin by pushing back their chair and standing.

Jesus did not escalate the anger. He could have gotten angry and confronted the Pharisees face to face. Instead, he helped de-escalate the situation by stooping down. I have stood up for my rights before, and all it got me was a black eye.

Can you sit down? Can you take the wind out of your sails? Can you ask people to think through the matter with cool heads and tender hearts instead of hot mouths? If you are easily lit or have a short fuse, you will diminish your ability to help others.

6.   Can you give truth and patience the time they need to work? The Pharisees were convicted by their own conscience when Jesus suggested that whoever was without blame cast the first stone. We would like to think that people can be convicted by our words. Notice that Jesus didn't call them hypocrites. Jesus didn't argue with them. He made one statement and allowed the truth to sink into their hearts.

Truth is rarely a quick fix; the people who want your counsel want an immediate fix. Your Biblical counsel might not be immediately heeded. Can you be patient enough for the truth to foment change within the person? It is God's job to change a person; it is not your job. You present the truth.

In my early years of counseling, I often felt that people had to see everything my way. The Bible taught me that the truth changes people; I do not. As a counselor, you need to say, "I appreciate your position. I gave you my position because you asked me for it. If you walk out of this office and disagree with me, I will respect you. I am not trying to convince you of my way; I am simply answering your question."

People might leave your office angry when you present the truth, but you must learn not to worry about their anger. If you present the truth and it angers someone, then you just need to give the truth time to be kneaded, as dough. Mentors allow the truth to take root until the conscience says, "I have to do something about this." You don't make them free; the truth is what makes people free.

7. Are you able to bring the matter to a conclusion? Well-meaning people have the problem of spreading a story and allowing the shame to live. People with knowledge of someone's sin can hold the matter against a person. The Pharisees were not trying to bring the matter to a conclusion. By bringing the woman into the midst of the temple, they let everyone in the temple know about her sin. Even though Jesus forgave the woman, the temple goers left with the knowledge of her adultery; thus, her sin would live on because more people knew about it. More people would give her the evil eye and disapproving looks.

Jesus beautifully said, "...*Neither do I condemn thee: go, and sin no more.*" He essentially said, "Are we done with this matter now? Good. Is this problem behind you now? It is? Great. I'm done with it, too." Jesus showed that the action is to fix the issue and not to expose the evil. Counselors must bring matters to a close. They must not remember sins against people.

The challenge of counseling is immense. There are no quick success stories. The stories are filled with patience, gentleness, and kindness. The stories are filled with rejection and heartbreak. There is little glory in counseling. Counselors are like the scientists who nurse wounded animals back to health and release them into the wild. For a short time they are needed, but if they properly train, they will never be needed again. Counseling is not for everyone. It is a job for the one who is willing to stand face to face with the depths of depravity—even in the lives of dear Christian brothers—and play the part of a savior.